PURE
WISDOM

Prentice Hall LIFE

If life is what you make it, then making it better starts here.

What we learn today can change our lives tomorrow. It can change our goals or change our minds; open up new opportunities or simply inspire us to make a difference. That's why we have created a new breed of books that do more to help you make more of *your* life.

Whether you want more confidence or less stress, a new skill or a different perspective, we've designed *Prentice Hall Life* books to help you to make a change for the better. Together with our authors we share a commitment to bring you the brightest ideas and best ways to manage your life, work and wealth.

In these pages we hope you'll find the ideas you need for the life *you* want. Go on, help yourself.

It's what you make it

* * *

PURE
WISDOM

The simple things that transform everyday life

DEAN CUNNINGHAM

Prentice Hall Life
is an imprint of

PEARSON

Harlow, England • London • New York • Boston • San Francisco • Toronto
Sydney • Tokyo • Singapore • Hong Kong • Seoul • Taipei • New Delhi
Cape Town • Madrid • Mexico City • Amsterdam • Munich • Paris • Milan

PEARSON EDUCATION LIMITED

Edinburgh Gate
Harlow CM20 2JE
Tel: +44 (0)1279 623623
Fax: +44 (0)1279 431059
Website: www.pearsoned.co.uk

First published in Great Britain in 2011

© Dean Cunningham 2011

The right of Dean Cunningham to be identified as author of this work has been asserted by him in accordance with the Copyright, Designs and Patents Act 1988.

ISBN: 978-0-273-74298-2

British Library Cataloguing-in-Publication Data
A catalogue record for this book is available from the British Library

Library of Congress Cataloging-in-Publication Data
Cunningham, Dean.
  Pure wisdom : the simple things that transform everyday life / Dean Cunningham.
    p. cm.
  ISBN 978-0-273-74298-2 (pbk.)
 1. Conduct of life. I. Title.

BJ1581.2.C86 2011
170'.44--dc22
                                                            2010053177

The publisher is grateful for permission to reproduce the photographs: Page 1 © Aaron Amat, 2011; Page 53 © Serg64, 2011; Page 105 © Mario7, 2011. All used under license from Shutterstock.

ARP Impression 98
Printed in Great Britain by Ashford Colour Press Ltd

Design by Design Deluxe
Typeset in 12pt Humanist 521 by 30

For three special women in my life,
my mum, sister and wife

Contents

PART THREE RIGHT UNDERSTANDING

Acknowledgements

Thanks to the many teachers, family, friends and foes who have helped me to learn some important lessons in life. Also thanks to editor Rachael Stock for making this book possible.

Introduction

*P*ure *Wisdom* takes a look at life beyond the way things appear to be.

Most of us rarely look twice. We get caught up in the flow of life. We live in haste and spend little time understanding what really matters. Without realising it, we settle for second best, we miss what's important and we don't live life to its fullest extent.

This simple but deeply insightful book helps us all to see things differently. It reveals the often overlooked things that make a difference to our experience of the world, and uses that knowledge to guide us to live a better and more fulfilling life.

Wisdom isn't a set of secrets accessible only to the intellectual elite, the most pious or religiously devout. Every one of us already shows signs of wisdom in our lives. This book will help you to see more clearly what you're doing when you act wisely. Armed with this knowledge you'll be in a better position to switch wisdom on when you need it most.

Pure Wisdom contains important fundamental principles that have the power to transform your life. But it relies on your ability to apply them skilfully to each unique situation or challenge. Each chapter will help you to develop that skill, but as with any activity in life, practice promotes improvement.

So what's the source of the wisdom in this book? It's the product of over a thousand years of ancient wisdom, distilled and applied to modern life through thirty years of martial arts training, conversations with masters, challenging life experiences and lessons learnt from developing others. Perhaps some of the biggest lessons I've learnt have come from karate. It's like a microcosm of life. And it provides countless lessons to improve it.

Karate has taught me you must first 'be' a certain type of person, then 'do' what you need to do, in order to 'have' what you want. Most people who practise karate get it backwards: they try to 'have' more of a thing (muscle, belts, power or whatever), in order to 'do' something (fight, win or impress other people) so that they can 'be' a thing (tough, fearless or a champion). But to master karate, 'being' must precede 'doing'.

Life is the same. Most people try to 'have' more of a thing (more money, more fame, more power, more status), in order to 'do' something (buy a faster car, a bigger house, another house), so that they can 'be' a thing (happy, successful, in love). But to master life, again 'being' must precede 'doing'.

That's why this book is organised into three parts (Right Attitude, Right Practice and Right Understanding), each containing twenty chapters about the attitudes, characteristics and behaviours needed to transform everyday life. You see, the right attitude leads to the right practice, which in turn leads to understanding and having the things that matter most in life – compassion, freedom, energy, peace, joy and wisdom, to name a few.

And finally, a warning …

Wisdom is full of contradictions. In one breath we say: 'Many hands make light work'. But in another we say: 'Too many cooks spoil the broth'. We claim: 'Absence makes the heart grow fonder'. Then we declare: 'Out of sight, out of mind'. The wise learn how to reconcile these contradictions, and many more. For example: when to act, and when to wait; when to give, and when to take; when to stay, and when to go. They know that the secret to a fulfilling life is a balanced life. In fact, wisdom begins with the art of balance, and, coincidentally, so does this book.

PART ONE

Right Attitude

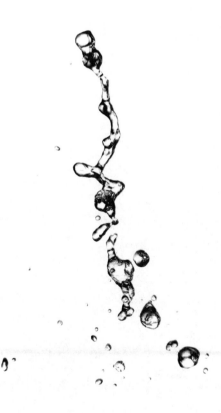

CHAPTER 1

Balanced

It's funny. When we hit on a good thing, we tend to think life is all about that thing. For instance: we get our dream job, and think life is all about our job. We experience the benefits of going to the gym, and think life is all about the gym. We notice the positive reactions we get when we have a haircut, and think life is all about our hairstyle.

For optimum benefit, however, everything you do in life needs to be balanced. Because if you went to the gym 7 days a week, you'd soon suffer from overtraining. If you worked a hundred hours a week, you'd soon burn out. And if you cut your hair every day, you'd soon be wearing a wig. Simply put: to get the most out of life, you need time to recover and space to grow.

> *To get the most out of life, you need time to recover and space to grow.*

In karate I see a lack of balance all the time. People think the harder, faster and longer they train the better they'll become. In a sense they're right — it takes hard work to master a skill. But they forget a fundamental lesson: if you want to move forward with force, you need stability. As a child, you couldn't learn how to ride a bike without stabilisers or a helping hand. You needed balance to move forwards. The same applies to all areas of life. No balance, no progress.

But let's not be unbalanced about being in balance. You see, the concept is often misunderstood. Most people think there's a happy medium where you can operate all of the time. And if you're not there, well, then you're doing something wrong. When in reality we will always be in and out of balance. Stand on one foot and you'll notice you continually have to make adjustments to stay there. Likewise, in life, you'll always have to make adjustments to stay where you want to be.

So instead of trying constantly to balance all areas of your life, acknowledge that anything important, and anything done well, will sometimes demand your full attention and pull you out of balance. At times it may be a demanding child or an unhappy partner, and your work will suffer. At other times it may be an important project, and fitness and relationships will be neglected. You see, balance isn't a constant state. There will always be times when you have to tip the scales between your commitments and passions.

Understand: there's nothing wrong with letting yourself get out of balance, as long as you can get yourself back. Just be careful not to be out of balance for too long – you might forget the difference. In other words: too much of a good thing can make you feel sick. But feeling sick can soon start to feel normal.

But that's not it. Balance isn't just about activity; it's about attitude too. For example: a healthy life requires us to balance the desire to change with the acceptance of who we are right now. It needs us to balance being persistent with letting go. And it requires us to balance self-discipline with freedom and spontaneity. In short: the key to a better, healthier and more successful life is simply this – balance.

CHAPTER 2

Calm

'Can you just calm down …'. Cue the explosion. Few people like to be told to calm down, especially when they're emotionally charged. Those words are like magic. They have the power to turn smouldering flames into an inferno. But even if you don't like being told to, there are major benefits to staying calm in emotional situations. And, not surprisingly, those benefits are seen most clearly in conflict.

As karate regularly demonstrates, if an opponent makes you upset, angry or mad they'll have an advantage. You see, angry fighters are tense fighters. Their reactions are slower. And their minds are clouded with emotions. In contrast, calm opponents have a daunting aura. Their unperturbed persona portrays strength and confidence. One look into their eyes is enough to make you doubt your ability.

Some people assume you need to get fired up to fight. But the complete opposite is true. In karate you soon learn to lose your temper permanently. Because, as with being relaxed, being calm provides a neutral position from which you can think and act. You see clearer, act faster and become a more formidable opponent. But being calm isn't all about knowing how to win a fight. There are benefits for everyday life too.

For example, when you're able to stay calm during emotional episodes, you're less likely to overreact and cause unnecessary damage to relationships. Make no mistake: there's nothing wrong with strong emotions; it's your response to them that counts. So if you're angry, for instance, you can choose to stay present with the experience of anger, let it pass, and decide how to respond when you're in a clearer headspace, rather than being reactive and out of control.

How? Acknowledge the emotion. Say to yourself: 'I feel angry', and then pay attention to the body sensations associated with it. If your mind wanders, bring it back to the body. This practice alone has the power to reduce the strength of the emotion. And in the calm space that this practice creates, you'll be less likely to overreact. What's more, there will be no need to deny your feelings or turn them inwards where they may accumulate.

> *If you lose your head you won't be able to use it.*

A calm mind is helpful in a crisis too. It's like being in the eye of a storm, totally untouched by the strong winds that surround you. In this position you can see right through the matter and make better decisions. It sounds obvious, but if you lose your head you won't be able to use it. So learn to stay calm under pressure. Now I'm aware some people will find it easier than others to adopt this way of being. Some personality types are more disposed to calmness than others. But we can all make improvements, no matter where we stand on the continuum.

Understand: you don't need to get swept away by your emotion. Stay still and let it unfold. No need to judge it. Just acknowledge it and watch it pass. And in the calm space you create, your action will be the most appropriate action. Not a reaction.

CHAPTER 3

Committed

For some people commitment is a terrifying word. It evokes the fear of being stuck in a bad relationship or trapped in an unfulfilling job. But there's more to commitment than a golden handcuff or platinum wedding band.

You see, to achieve anything of significance in life you need commitment. Like a professional athlete you have to decide that you want to be your best, give your best, and make the pursuit of self-improvement a priority. Come rain or shine, athletes turn up. If they're feeling tired, they turn up. If they'd rather be doing something else on that particular day, they still show up.

Athletes understand that commitment doesn't guarantee success, but without it they might not get out of the starting blocks, let alone complete the race. And so when they train, they train with commitment. They stay focused. They're there for a reason. They give everything they've got. Because they know if they're not committed they'll be at a disadvantage. It's the same in life. No commitment. No progress. And no results.

You may have a dream or goal but are you committed? Commitment is an inner drive and determination to complete your goal. It's not something you can manufacture. It's either there, or it's not. You see, commitment depends on the value that you place on your goal. If it's not that important to you, you won't be committed. It's the same with jobs and relationships. If you don't value them, you won't be in them for long. So if you're struggling to commit to a person, position or path, ask yourself this: 'Am I sure this is what I really want?'. If you're not, don't waste your time.

If it is what you want, but you're still struggling to commit, then you're not alone. Some people find it hard to commit to anything. If that sounds like you, try to understand the underlying reason. Get in touch with the feelings and thoughts that hold you back. Do you fear being rejected, hurt or restricted? Are your thoughts rational? Remember: commitment comes from the heart and not the head, or another human. So don't let irrational thoughts or other people hold you back. Only you know what is important to you. And you're the only one who should decide your commitments. What's more, if you're not feeling it you'll easily be distracted by temptations: a drink, a dress, a dessert or whatever. So follow your heart.

> *When you're committed there are no shortcuts, no easy path. You don't leave yourself an escape hatch.*

When you're committed there are no shortcuts, no easy path. You don't leave yourself an escape hatch. It's like a rollercoaster. Once you're in, you're in. You have to ride it until the end. It takes grit and determination to honour your commitments. But that's exactly what turns a dream into a reality.

Understand: commitments should always be realistic and achievable. So don't be too ambitious. Start slowly. Increase them bit by bit. Soon you'll develop a routine or habit and your commitments will become a way of life.

CHAPTER 4

Compassionate

M ost of us have been there. Somebody says something really hurtful and, before you know it, you've lashed out back at them. Either that or gone away to hide in a corner. Anger or anxiety; fight or flight. It's all down to basic instincts. When you feel you're under attack (and that could be emotionally, verbally or physically) most people attack back, or run away. It's deeply ingrained. But a more evolved response would be to show compassion.

> *Most people are hurting, what they need is healing, not another beating.*

Most people you meet are fighting a difficult battle. They're battling with stressful jobs, unfulfilling jobs, difficult relationships, financial troubles or ill health. Few of us get through life without a major difficultly. Most people are hurting. And let's face it: hurting people hurt people. So be kind. What they need is healing, not another beating. It's tough, I know, especially when you've been hurt by the person you want to be kind to. But remember, compassion is the ability to treat people better than (you think) they deserve.

But don't get me wrong. I'm not saying you should put up with abuse. If someone is attacking you, defend yourself. Kindness doesn't mean weakness. So take appropriate action, but be compassionate. I guess the key word here is 'appropriate' because if (figuratively speaking) you can warn off an aggressor with a firm hand, why use a fist?

That's not all. You need to understand this: kindness begets kindness. Take holidays, for example. When we're relaxed and on holiday we become friendlier and more generous. And more often than not the locals reciprocate our kindness and generosity. We come away thinking great things about the people in the country we visited, and wonder why the folks back home aren't the same. But we fail to see the part we played in the treatment we received. Life at home can be like a holiday too if we learn to be kind, friendly and warm.

And, remember, compassion for others begins with compassion for yourself. So talk to yourself in nurturing ways. Be kind. Treat yourself with the same care and attention you would hope for from others. Then when you've mastered that stage, spread your kindness to people you care about, people you feel neutral about, and people you can't stand.

CHAPTER 5

Confident

We're often told to aim high. But more often than not we set goals that are too hard rather than too easy. The problem is, if we're out of our depth or experience consistent failure we erode our confidence. The typical solution is to set goals that stretch us but are achievable. For example: if we know we can manage only 10 push-ups, there'd be little point in setting a goal to do twenty. So we set a target we can achieve, say eleven, in the hope that our confidence will benefit from the success. Sounds like a sensible idea. But, as you'll see, success isn't the best way to build confidence.

> **Confidence is contagious.**

Observing others performing well can build confidence too. To improve my karate techniques I have spent hours watching video footage of world karate champions. Seeing the best in action is a brilliant source of inspiration. So if you want to be more confident when, for example, speaking in public, meeting new people or facing an opponent, watch others and copy them. Confidence is contagious.

Add verbal persuasion to vicarious experience and you'll soon be well on your way to a more decisive and determined attitude. You see, words have the power to build confidence. Watch any major sports event and you'll see what I mean. Athletes are always talking to themselves. They curse when things go wrong and shout in jubilation when things go their way. You can use this technique too. The trick is to find words and phrases that work for you. Statements that evoke positive emotions are best. So if 'I can't afford to fail' makes you feel nervous and on edge, then try something different, such as: 'Stick to the plan, do your best and you'll be fine'.

If these how-to steps are still not enough to increase your levels of confidence then perhaps you need a better understanding of who you are. Let me explain. For most of us confidence is built on successful outcomes. So when we fail to achieve something important we tend to equate this failure with failure as a person. We lose confidence. And that's because we think we are defined by our behaviour. But we're not. Take a closer look at yourself and you'll notice you consist of a number of aspects. Yes, you are your behaviour. But you're also your thoughts, feelings, characteristics, memories and body parts too. And not one of those aspects is permanent. Not even your memories are consistent. Who you are as a person is constantly changing. So does it make sense to judge yourself as a failure with such a narrow measure? I think not.

In any case, if your confidence is built on your actions and the subsequent outcomes – a title, a qualification, a spouse or any other prize – then it's standing on shaky ground. You see, confidence isn't all about being successful. Genuine confidence is built on knowing you're like every other human being on this planet: fallible, unique and constantly changing. Sure, parts of who you are may be different, better or worse than another person. For example: you may be a better cook; they may be a better teacher. You may be a great listener; they might have a way with words. But that doesn't make you superior or inferior to them.

> *Genuine confidence is built on knowing you're fallible, unique and constantly changing.*

Understand: genuine confidence isn't built on success alone. And it can't be undermined by external circumstances – the way you look, failures, mistakes or other people's opinions. So accept yourself unconditionally and your confidence will be as firm as the ground you stand on.

CHAPTER 6

Courageous

In order to learn karate, at some point you've got to fight a real person. Karate isn't keep-fit combat – it's get-hit combat. So eventually you have to confront the fear of getting hurt.

Let's face it: people don't want to get hurt. But in karate you can't let this fear stop you. You've got to move forward and strike. So you learn how to control the fear: you develop a plan of action, you know exactly what you'll do if your partner counterattacks, and you move towards the thing you fear. If you don't, you give up. But giving up isn't a real option. Not if you plan on attaining a black belt or mastering your art.

Imagine if you gave up learning to walk because you feared falling and getting a bruised bum. Think about how limited your life would be, the experiences you would miss. Sounds ridiculous, I know. The strange thing is people give up all the time because they fear being bruised by failure, criticism and rejection. But a successful life follows countless rejections, criticisms and failures. When you were in nappies each attempt you made to walk led to a failure. You weren't aware of it at the time, but each outcome provided you with the feedback you needed to learn how to walk. Each failure took you one step closer to living a fuller life.

Life is full of risks. So to achieve anything worthwhile you'll always have something to fear. In karate, you learn quickly to abandon the search for complete security and safety. No matter how carefully you practise, you'll always get a black eye or bruised toe. Life is the same: no matter how well you plan, it presents you with a continuous succession of problems, disappointments and obstacles. The only time you'll find real safety and security on this earth is when you're buried six feet deep under it.

Everyone is afraid of something – even black belts in karate. But nobody needs to know you're afraid. In a real fight, if your opponent smells blood you'll soon be licking it off your top lip. So keep your fears to yourself, but share your courage with others. Get very clear: courage isn't the absence of fear, but the conquest of it.

> *Courage isn't the absence of fear, but the conquest of it.*

Understand: life will present you with lessons and those lessons never run out. So don't complain, make excuses, or wish that somehow things could be easier or safer. Look for the lesson and don't be scared to go out on a limb: that's where the fruit is. It's all right to be cautious but remember, not even a turtle gets anywhere until he sticks his head out.

CHAPTER 7

Creative

To solve any problem in life you need to be creative. Because as the old saying goes: if you continue to do the same things, you'll always get the same results. But being creative can be a daunting task. Give most people a blank sheet of paper, figuratively or actually, to start the creative process and they'll finish with a blank mind. But being creative doesn't necessarily mean coming up with original ideas. In fact, most new ideas are combinations of old ones with a fresh wrapping. The good news is there are some useful questions that can help you to generate life-changing ideas. But before I share them with you, let me say this.

We often fail to solve problems because we fail to think outside the box. Our habitual actions and ways of thinking restrain our creativity. But, to live a more fulfilling life, we need to break free from our set ways of doing things. We need to look at life from different angles. In a sense, we need to grow up. You see, as children we learnt how to behave by copying the people around us. As adults we copy others to learn new skills too. But there comes a point in our development when we have to stop copying.

As a Japanese master once told me: 'To master karate, you must first imitate your teacher. But at some point you must go beyond what you've been taught and create your own techniques'. You see, imitation is necessary in the early stages of learning but it lacks creativity. Eventually we must transcend what is known and develop our craft. That's the way to grow. Essentially, techniques are stepping-stones to a place where we can be creative. When we get to that place in karate our activity transforms from a science into an art.

> ## *There comes a point when we have to break free from copying.*

It's the same in life: we learn ways of living that serve a purpose at our early stages, but when we find ourselves in new situations the old behaviour tends not to work. There comes a point when we need to drop the old method, move on, adopt new behaviour and reach new heights. Here's how.

First, you need to know what you want – the end result. The critical questions are: what do I want to create? and what do I want to happen? Next you need to know what exists currently. Ask: what is my present situation? and what is happening now? Then you need to be creative. The following questions are guaranteed to get your creative juices flowing. What would a person I admire do? How else could a person handle this? What would be the proactive thing to do? What would I do if I moved towards the fear? Then, when you've explored enough options, pick one and take action.

Once you get your creative muscles pumping, ideas will come freely and naturally. But the key is to capture the good ones and use them. Remember: insight is useless without action.

CHAPTER 8

Disciplined

We've all been given a wonderful gift in life: our free will. I see that gift as being synonymous to a steering wheel. It's our free 'wheel' to steer the course we wish to travel in life; our free 'wheel' to make choices and take different roads; our free 'wheel' to take an active and not passive role on our journey.

For most of us, though, it's as if we're asleep at the wheel, on automatic pilot, letting our default map, which is made up of our habitual actions, guide us to the same places even when we no longer want to go there. In a sense, we've lost grip of our wheel – we stay in the same old job we hate or join gyms with the intention of getting into shape but never turn up. But to fulfil your dreams you need to get a grip on your wheel, hold it firmly in your hands, and steer your life in the direction of your choice.

> **Discipline is what separates where we are now from where we want to be.**

It takes discipline or 'wheel-power' to override our habitual behaviour. In sport, discipline is what separates an amateur from a pro. In life, it's what separates where we are now from where we want to be.

Most people define discipline as 'control' – being told what to do by an authority, 'punishment' – being put on a performance plan at work, or 'doing without' – refusing a glass of wine at dinner. But discipline isn't always imposed on us. Sometimes it's a tool we use to get the things we want. In fact, we all demonstrate discipline on a daily basis. We brush our teeth, shower, and go to work. Then we come home, slump in front of the TV, and make a disciplined effort to keep up with our favourite show.

Clearly we all have a degree of discipline, but most of us need to develop it to reach our more significant goals. It's equivalent to trying to strengthen a muscle. It's a case of use it, or lose it. With frequent use it becomes stronger. If it's neglected, it becomes as useless as a withered muscle that's been wrapped in a plaster cast for a month.

Now that might sound obvious. But what most people fail to understand is, when we set goals we tend to leap enthusiastically into our new way of living. It's like trying to lift the heaviest weights in the gym on our first visit. Unconditioned muscles couldn't bear the weight. Likewise, unconditioned discipline will collapse under the weight of our commitments. So, if you want to eat more healthily, for example, begin by making small changes to your diet rather than leaping into zero salt, zero sugar and no caffeine.

As with exercising a muscle, what we need to do is start out sensibly, take on one task at a time, push through the initial discomfort, slowly increase the challenge and acknowledge our gradual improvement. That's how you cultivate discipline.

CHAPTER 9

Fearless

Fear has an acrostic: False Evidence Appearing Real. It's often quoted to help people banish their imaginary fears. Clever and creative in its construction, it is often misunderstood in its application. Let me explain.

Essentially, there are two kinds of fear. One kind is the feeling we get when we're physically threatened. It's the feeling we have if we're about to be run over by a car when crossing the road. It's the kind of fear that shouts: run, dodge, dive or get out of the way. Clearly there's nothing imaginary about that, and no need for the acrostic.

The other kind of fear is in our heads. It's the thoughts we hold about what might happen in the future, based on our imagination or experiences in the past. This is the type of fear the acrostic is aimed at.

The trouble is, people often interpret the acrostic this way: if the fear is not an immediate physical threat, it's not real. But I disagree. Fear's function is to stop you from getting hurt. It warns you of danger whether it's a few months away, just around the corner or in your face. For instance, if I'm going to fight in a karate tournament next week and I know I've got holes in my defence, of course I'm going to be afraid. Especially when the symmetry of my nose is at stake. In fact, I'd probably pull out of the competition or work on my blocking skills. Fear of the future is helpful, healthy even. It motivates you to take action.

You see, fear isn't the problem; it's the thought behind the fear. For example: if each time you took a lift you worried about it getting stuck, even when you had no evidence to prove it would, that would be unhealthy. Just a minute: I take that back. It may be healthy if you ended up taking the stairs. But it would be impractical if you had 30 floors to climb.

On a serious note, be very clear, we're not talking about being fearless here. The point is: we need to uncover the thought behind the fear, and then evaluate the evidence. If the evidence is false, then so is the fear.

> *We don't need to be fearless. We just need to fear less.*

There's more. We sometimes fear the unknown, or imagine things will be worse than they turn out to be. But, again, this doesn't mean we should be fearless. The right amount of fear is a good thing. It gets you moving. It invites you to choose differently. It might even get you up a flight of stairs. But when fear is taken out of the moment, held onto with a tight grip, that's when fear becomes a problem. It loses its motivational impact. It keeps you stuck rather than safe.

By now I guess you're saying: 'This chapter isn't about being fearless'. And you're right. It's not. Fear is such a powerful emotion that trying to get rid of it would be a waste of time. Even a clever acrostic, like the one above, wouldn't be much help in that pursuit. I'm no fearless warrior. Never was. Never will be. And don't care to be. In fact karate teaches: we don't need to be fearless. We just need to fear less.

How? Listen to the fear. Learn the lesson. Take appropriate action. Then let go and move on.

CHAPTER 10

Flexible

In karate, doing the splits is a common way to demonstrate flexibility. And for some newcomers it's a goal that provides the motivation to train. No doubt, the splits is a sign of brilliant mobility and supple muscles, both of which are important for executing karate techniques. But there's more to flexibility than stretching your legs. Flexibility protects the body. It's healthy. If muscles are tense and rigid they become susceptible to strains and chronic pain. So it pays to keep them supple.

Nevertheless, karate isn't all about physical flexibility. Flexibility of the mind is important too. You see, in a fight the mind needs to be fluid and responsive. A tense and rigid mind would put you at a major disadvantage. In life a fixed and unyielding mind has its dangers too. When the mind is inflexible it becomes unbalanced and vulnerable to emotional pain. So it pays to keep it flexible.

The trouble is when it comes to our preferences in life we have a tendency to take a rigid stance. We lose our flexibility and end up getting hurt. But for better emotional health we need to be responsive to life and the changes it demands. Even if that means letting go of our desires and preferences. For example, most people believe life shouldn't be painful.

But a more flexible attitude would be: 'It would be great if life was pain free, but pain is an inevitable part of human life'. And here's another example: many people believe they're entitled to rewards for their hard work or good behaviour. Flex that and you get: 'Life is not always fair. Sometimes you'll put in the work and not get what you want'. I could go on but I'm sure you get the picture.

> **We need to be responsive to life and the changes it demands.**

The point: we need to see when it's wise to change our mind and let go of our preferences and fixed notions. The good thing is our language is littered with clues. If you express a 'must' or absolute 'should' then it's a sure sign of a rigid position. To loosen up, open to the possibility of things not happening the way you would prefer or look for new approaches. So if you find yourself saying: 'This is the way it "should" be done', take that as your cue to ask: 'I wonder what other approach I could take – and which would work best?'. Learn to move with the flow of life. Consider changing your opinion and be open to new opportunities. That's how to be flexible.

CHAPTER 11

Grateful

Most of us have grown up with parents who taught us to be grateful. They told us to be thankful for the food on the table, the roof over our head and for our good health. As a child, you probably didn't pay much attention to gratitude. I know I didn't. If I wanted the latest pair of trainers, the 'you should be grateful that you have trainers to wear' or 'think about the people who don't have any feet' perspective didn't pack a big enough punch to drum the point home.

Sure, I had enough empathy to feel sorry for a person without feet. But in my world I didn't run into enough of them to make me realise how lucky I was to have my own. I rarely saw their frustrations and I didn't feel their pain. So that line of thought didn't work for me. I took my feet for granted. What's more, I still wanted a new pair of trainers.

Now I have a better understanding of how the mind works, I can see the importance of being thankful. You see, when you appreciate something, you turn your attention to it. And, as I now know, what you pay attention to conditions your thinking, creates your perceptions and controls your experience of reality. From this perspective, an attitude of gratitude certainly makes sense. It keeps your attention focused on what you have and less on what you want. When you make it a habit to fix your attention on what you have, life becomes full – you feel fulfilled.

> **When you appreciate something, you turn your attention to it.**

Often we don't make complete use of the things we own. We constantly chase what's new even when what we possess doesn't need replacing. But that doesn't matter to us. We must have the latest, newest and best. But if we don't enjoy what we already have, how on earth are we going to be happier with more?

Being grateful isn't all about material things. We need to be grateful for life situations too. In karate we are trained to show our appreciation regularly. After each activity with a partner or an opponent we bow and say thank you in Japanese. From an outside perspective it must look strange to see a person thank their opponent for a good beating. You just knocked the wind out of me. Thank you. Thank you for my sore lip. Sounds crazy, I know. But we're learning to be thankful for the rough and the smooth. It's the tough fights that raise our level. It's the same in life. Perversely, we should be grateful for the hard times that come our way. They bring out the best in us.

CHAPTER 12

Honest

Do you lie? Let's face it, we all do. You may not tell blatant lies, but we all make slight distortions of the truth, all-day and every day. For many, white lies are acceptable, but blatant lying – no way! Clearly there are some good reasons to hide the truth, but more often than not there are better reasons to be honest.

> *Clearly there are some good reasons to hide the truth, but more often than not there are better reasons to be honest.*

Being found out is an obvious downside to lying. But there are many other sensible reasons not to lie. For instance, you won't have to cover your tracks. Constantly covering your tracks saps your energy. Plus, once you get the reputation of being someone who tells the truth, people will listen to you because they know they can trust you. What's more, when you can admit you're wrong and own up to your mistakes it's hard for a person to criticise you. You gain a lot of respect for being honest.

No doubt there are people who rise up the ranks of success on the back of dishonesty. But more often than not they get found out. And the higher they rise the harder they fall – usually bringing others down with them.

So why do we lie? Lying starts in childhood as a defence mechanism against figures of authority who are usually intimidating. Teachers ask: 'Did you do your homework?'. We answer: 'Uh, yes I did, but I left it at home'. Then to us as adults, police ask: 'Do you know how fast you were driving?'. We answer: 'I guess I was doing forty'. And when we're told we were driving over the limit, we profess: 'I didn't know I was going that fast'.

Often we lie because we're afraid of the consequences of telling the truth. Or sometimes we're dishonest because we think the truth will hurt others. But how do you feel when you know you're not being told the truth? Most people yearn for straight talk. We all respect honest people. Telling the truth, tactfully, builds better relationships than lying, holding back or distorting the facts.

Honesty starts right here – with you. But it's surprising how difficult it is to accept the truth about yourself. Are you honest with yourself? I mean really honest. How do you handle feedback? Do you get defensive? And if you're honest with yourself, are you able to tell that truth about yourself to another? How do you handle compliments? Do you disagree or express appreciation? Are you able to admit your mistakes? When you're made aware of a weakness can you express appreciation for the messenger and communicate genuine enthusiasm about making a change?

But that's not all there is to being honest. Do you tell other people what you think they want to hear or the truth? Honest feedback is a gift, if you have the right intentions. But be tactful. Telling it like it is can be counterproductive.

When in doubt, tell the truth.

The ultimate goal is never to lie. But, of course, there are times when it would not be professional or discreet to reveal all. However, statements such as 'I'm not able to discuss that right now. When I can, I will', or 'Sorry, this is not something I feel comfortable talking about', reinforce your integrity. Make this your motto: when in doubt, tell the truth. It's simple but it'll have a favourable impact on your life.

CHAPTER 13

Meticulous

Being meticulous is about paying attention to small details. As a hugely successful world karate champion once told me, attention to detail is what separates him from the rest. Successful people in many walks of life understand the importance of detail. You see, they know the biggest differences emerge from making a lot of little differences – to the details.

Focus on the small details during a physical workout and you'll be surprised how quickly you become exhausted. It's tough. But working out in this way leads to great leaps in progress. In a few short sessions you begin to see your overall performance improve. In a real sense: when you sweat the small stuff, you enhance the big stuff.

In karate details are important. When we train we focus our attention on each movement. We seek to perform every technique with care and attention. Karate masters know the value of doing things thoroughly to completion. They have a thirst for perfection and finesse. And they understand that when they practise in this way they're not only training their body, they're also training their mind. It's the same in all areas of life. Paying attention to the details leads to small improvements that add up to make a big difference. Not only physically, but mentally too.

Want a quick win? Fix the details. You can always do something about the details. It's something you can instantly improve. It's like straightening your tie: one small adjustment makes all the difference. So look for small things to improve. Do what's doable. You'll build momentum and feel like you're actually getting somewhere.

So if you want to improve your public speaking skills, for example, pay attention to the details. Make every word count. Become aware of your mannerisms and drop the ones that cause a distraction. Mean what you say, and mean it when you move. Understand your audience and fulfil their needs in small but significant ways. Adjust the temperature of the room. Set the lighting. Fix the sound.

> *The brilliance behind every outstanding piece of work or performance is always found in the smallest of details.*

The brilliance behind every outstanding piece of work or performance is always found in the smallest of details. Surgeons know it. Computer programmers know it. Athletes know it. Engineers know it. Writers know it. Photographers know it. Business people know it. Designers know it. Artists know it. They all understand the secret to quality in every aspect of their work is doing the little things well. Precision. Attention to detail. Perfection. That's what being meticulous is all about.

CHAPTER 14

Mindful

Paradoxically, the most driven and successful people are often the most dissatisfied. Why? Well, to be successful in life you need to be a go-getter, a doer. You need good judgment, a logical mind and great problem-solving skills. What's more, you need the ability to evaluate where you are now and where you want to be. Then, you need the drive and determination to close that gap. All these skills are highly regarded and essential for a successful life 'out there', but when it comes to a successful life 'in here' they aren't always so helpful. In fact, they can make matters worse.

Let me explain.

In the pursuit of a better life most people forget that, in the end, everything we do is motivated by a desire to attain an internal state: contentment, satisfaction and fulfilment. What's more, we forget that the stuff we achieve 'out there' won't guarantee this state. In fact, there will always be gaps to close. So we push on, frantically chasing things – money, fame, power and status – but we never seem to be satisfied. We always want more stuff. But it's never enough. It never leads to lasting fulfilment.

But even if we understand that 'more' is not going to make us feel better, we make matters worse by trying to solve the problems 'in here' in the same way that we solve problems 'out there'. And if we're a whiz at solving 'outer' problems we're going to be a mess if we apply the same strategies to our 'inner' life.

You see, problem solving isn't the best way to handle emotional issues. Why? Because it makes us think repeatedly about the very things that caused the problem in the first place. We just keep going around in circles, rehashing the same experience, in a desperate attempt to find a way out of our misery.

But there is a way out, another mode of mind, which is the opposite of the goal-driven, gap-closing mind. It's the 'being' mode. And, in contrast to the 'doing' mode, it isn't motivated to achieve a particular goal. So there's no need for the constant review of the gap, assessing how things are with how we would like them to be, which makes us feel bad. Instead our focus is on 'accepting' and 'allowing' things to be as they are right now, without fantasising, yearning or hoping for something different.

Furthermore, the 'being' mode of mind encourages us to 'approach' rather than 'avoid' unwelcome emotional states, so we overcome our emotional challenges in a healthy way. Driving forward and ignoring the uncomfortable feeling is not going to make it go away. For a more satisfying life, at some point you'll have to face the discomfort and get to the root cause of it. The 'being' mode of mind can help.

You see, the 'being' mode encourages you to stop doing stuff and pay full attention to your current situation. It helps you to see more clearly, consider all possibilities, and make better decisions. It enables you to respond consciously instead of always operating on automatic pilot. When you're fully awake, you notice who you really are and what you really need. You break free of your addiction to 'more'. And you close the gap between external success and internal satisfaction.

> *When you're fully awake, you notice who you really are and what you really need.*

So how do we switch from the 'doing' mode of mind to the 'being' mode? The simplest way is to be mindful of the body. Because coming back to the sensations in our body brings us back to the present moment. But be careful not to turn this practice into a goal – achieving a state of calm or relaxation. What you're aiming to do is become more open to what you're experiencing in your body – right here, right now – no matter what that is.

Here's a good start: sit up in a comfortable posture. Place your legs and arms in a relaxed but fixed position. Close your eyes. Bring your mind to each part of your body. Start from the bottom, up. Take it slowly. Step by step. Body part by body part. So if you start with your left foot, put your mind there, become 'mindfoot'. I know, cheesy, but what else would you expect from a foot? There really is no need to get too serious with this stuff. Approach it with an attitude of lightheartedness, curiosity, warmth and kindness. That's the mindful way.

CHAPTER 15

Non-judgemental

We all have preferences. And there'll always be some things that we'll consider to be better than others. For example, you might prefer rum and raisin ice cream. I might prefer plain vanilla. We have different tastes. Fine. But only if … You see, we just can't seem to accept other people may not share our opinion. So we judge their choice: 'How could you eat that? It's awful'. And we try to convert them: 'You don't know what you're missing. Try this'. But for better relationships and peace of mind we need to understand that what is better for us might be worse for someone else.

Now I know the above example may sound trivial. I'm sure most people don't care about what others think when it comes to their choice of ice cream. It's a little more irritating, however, when we're being judged on our view of the world. But no matter how we feel about being judged we still find it difficult not to judge others. We believe our way is the best way. But what's right for us is not necessarily right for everyone.

Most of us have opinions about what other people should do to get out of a difficult situation or to make their life better. We say, 'I would never do that …'. But how do we know if we've never been in that same situation? Can we be sure we would act differently? Often we're no better than a back-seat driver.

We judge and criticise other people's actions when we've never been in the hot seat.

I'm sure you want the best for the people you care about most. You want to give them the 'best' advice. But that advice is usually based on your preferences. For example, you may want others to spend how you spend, eat how you eat, live how you live and believe what you believe. But your preferences are your preferences. In the end, they might not be the best things for yourself, let alone another. So let others do what they think is right for themselves. They may make bad choices but that's how people learn. Let them make their mistakes. And focus on learning from your own.

Understand: we can't always see the benefits that will come from another person's experience. We might judge it as being 'not right' but it could be right up their street. In other words, where people find themselves in this moment may be the perfect place for them, given where they are heading.

> *When you give advice to someone who hasn't asked for it, it isn't advice-giving, it's judging.*

What's more, when you give advice to someone who hasn't asked for it, it isn't advice-giving, it's judging. It'll be taken as a criticism. And criticisms disconnect relationships. Allow another to be, and they'll want to be around you. It's not often a person is made to feel accepted for who they are. Remember, nobody is perfect. And others will always be far from it, especially if they have to live up to your definition of the word.

CHAPTER 16

Open-minded

You may have heard the story of the Zen master who is confronted with a student who is full of himself: full of his ideas, concepts and beliefs; inflexible and reluctant to let go of his perspective. So the master sits him down and prepares tea. In a Zen-like manner the master pours himself a cup. Then he proceeds to pour a cup for the student. But this time he doesn't come to a measured stop. Instead he keeps pouring and allows the cup to overflow. In a panic, the student exclaims: 'Master, what are you doing?'. Calmly, the master replies: 'The cup is like your mind. You'll never be able to learn anything new unless you empty it.'

That's old wisdom. Here's a new understanding.

Sense organs – the skin, eyes, ears, tongue and nose – are instruments we use to navigate our journey through life. They act as receivers that provide us with information about the external world. Left to their own devices we would be overloaded with stimulus. But we have developed a clever way to prevent the multitude of sensations from overwhelming us. We search out what is interesting then we generalise, delete and distort the information we receive. Put simply, like a designer drug we customise our experience.

The trouble is our filtering system is influenced by our thoughts. And more often than we might realise, our thoughts are irrational. So we generalise about people and their characteristics and expect only the worse from them, delete important information that we need to pay attention to, or distort the meaning of what people say and respond inappropriately.

But that's not all. It gets worse. You see, we have a bad habit of looking for information that agrees with our way of thinking. So not only do our thoughts shape our reality, they confirm it too – no matter how twisted that reality might be. And, let's face it, it feels good to be right. So habitually we avoid people and facts that are not in agreement with our thoughts.

Again and again you've heard the cynical saying: 'Seeing is believing'. But it would be more accurate to say: 'Believing is seeing'. Because your perceptions of the world are always based on your habitual thoughts – your beliefs. They create the road map by which you steer your course through life. Think healthy, rational thoughts and they will lead you to where you want to be. Think unhealthy, inflexible thoughts and expect to hit a brick wall.

That's the problem.

Now here's the solution: be open-minded. See things as if you're seeing them for the first time. Empty your cup. Put aside your ideas, concepts and beliefs. And, as best you can, connect with the raw sensory data entering your brain. Think about what you're thinking. Look for people and literature that express a different opinion from yours. Then hunt for the facts that support their view. Understand: digging for facts is better mental exercise than jumping to conclusions.

> *Digging for facts is better mental exercise than jumping to conclusions.*

Make no mistake. I'm not asking you to throw out your opinions or compromise your values. Not at all. What I'm suggesting is to suspend focusing on and expressing your opinions until you have fully researched, listened to and understood other views. Then you'll be able to operate from a more balanced position. And, what's more, you'll be less likely to be deluded, diverted or driven down a dead-end.

CHAPTER 17

Patient

Patience is a desirable quality but in our culture of instant gratification it's a rare one. Don't get me wrong, it's great that we have twenty-four-hour shopping, microwave ovens, immediate access to information and entertainment on demand. But having access to what we want, when we want is weakening one of our greatest attributes – the ability to wait.

Research has shown that when children were given a choice of having one marshmallow now or two after completing a task, the children who were able to wait were more successful later in life. Having the ability to resist impulses matters. We may be born with different levels of patience. But we can all make improvements. It's like any other skill; it can be developed with practice.

It's not easy. Even the best of us have to resist the need for speedy gratification. We speed up to beat the traffic lights. We speed up to get to the shortest queue. And even when we can't move faster, we hurry in the mind. It's as if we are on a drug. We get addicted to speed. But for a better and more fulfilling life we need to break the addiction. We need to fight against the quick-hit mentality.

Understand: if patience is a virtue, get-on-demand is a vice. So don't be seduced by the cash-and-carry rush-and-hurry lifestyle. We're fortunate to have most of what we want on demand. But don't let that weaken your ability to delay gratification. If you're lacking patience begin to build it with small things. Waiting in a queue on the phone, for example, is a good training ground. When you're able to wait without being annoyed about or anxious with the small things, move on to the big.

And there's more. You see, the desire to get things done quickly often means they don't get done properly. So if you want great results, be patient. Even learning to be patient takes patience. You can't speed up the process. If you do, the product will not be the same. It'll be of a lesser quality. Speeding up personal development is like cracking an egg before it's ready to hatch. And then wondering why you didn't get a chick.

> **Patience is your willingness to let life move forward at its own pace.**

Keep this in mind: patience is your willingness to let life move forward at its own pace. There's no need to rush, push or hurry. Plant the seeds and let the organic process unfold. In other words, if you put in the effort you will see the fruits. They might not come when you want, but they will come when you're ready. And remember: the deeper the waiting, the sooner they'll come.

CHAPTER 18

Persistent

Persistence is the ability to stick with a task when the going gets tough. We all know people who start activities and stop as soon as they face an obstacle. I see it all the time in karate. Students start with enthusiasm, but it's awkward at first, and results come slowly, so they give up. They walk out just when things are about to get better.

Most people quit in life. They don't have the 'stick-to-it-ness' required to achieve their goals. Perhaps it's the quick-results mindset that holds them back. For example, it's not uncommon for novice karate students to expect to be a master in a minute. Nowadays people want instant results. But real progress comes with endless repetition and a concerted effort towards improvement. You see, it takes time and hard work to master a skill. There are no shortcuts. So if you don't have the time, don't expect the results.

Patience and persistence go hand in hand. They're like the ying and yang of commitment. Patience is the passive quality and persistence the more active. If you want to get ahead of the pack, stick with your pursuit until the end. That's the active part of commitment. Then don't be put off if the result isn't immediately visible. That's the passive element. It doesn't matter how slowly you're improving, the important thing is to keep going. Practise even when you feel like you're getting nowhere. That's the way to be your very best. Understand: the result will come, probably when you least expect it. So stick to your task.

> *Patience and persistence go hand in hand. They're like the ying and yang of commitment.*

All that said, it's important not to get out of balance with this principle. Sometimes you need to know when to quit. If your efforts make you feel like you're moving backwards as opposed to moving forward, or standing still, then that's a signal to get some rest. If rest doesn't lead to recovery, then perhaps you're on the wrong path. Consider alternative activities that are better suited to your natural talents.

No doubt, if you're ambitious and driven, knowing when to give up won't be easy. But don't let pride or stubbornness get in your way. Ask yourself honestly if you are quitting for the right or wrong reasons – then you'll know. Sure, people don't want to be quitters. But there's no point persisting with an activity that's not right for you.

CHAPTER 19

Respectful

Respect is accepting a person for what they are, whether you agree with that or not. For example, you might not agree with a person's political views, their religious beliefs or perspective on life. You might even disapprove of their actions and behaviour. But that doesn't mean you can't respect them. You don't have to admire a person or approve of their way of life to treat them with kindness and care.

> *Respect is accepting a person for what they are, whether you agree with that or not.*

Perhaps easy to understand, this principle is a tough one to follow. You see, we all tend to treat people we dislike with less respect. They just don't seem to be worth the effort. But it will always benefit our personal well-being if we can drop any grudges and allow people to be the way they are. If that's too much of a stretch, however, then at least try not to let others know you dislike them.

Sure, it's hard to pretend that you like someone when you blatantly don't. No one wants to be a fake. But in the end it's your problem, because everyone, no matter who they are, deserves to be treated with dignity and respect. Whether you truly like them or not, when you have a problem with another speak about it as *your* problem. That's not to say you have to agree with the other person to make them feel good. If you've got an opposing opinion, express it ... but be respectful.

Here's how.

Choose the most appropriate time to have the conversation. Communicate face to face, ideally, and use warm vocal tones. Begin by acknowledging the other person's point of view. For example, say: 'I understand and respect what you're saying, but here's another way of looking at it ...'. Then explain your opinion by stating the facts as you see them and how they make you feel.

Remember, we've all been exposed to a variety of experiences in life and have been cultured by our environments. Each one of us will therefore have a unique way of seeing the world. For example: you may have been raised in the Far East and believe that courtesies and protocols are important; in contrast, a person raised in the West may feel these things are largely unnecessary. We don't have to agree with everything a person says or believes, but at the same time, we don't have to verbally bite their head off when we don't.

CHAPTER 20

Responsible

It's a never-ending debate. Are we responsible for our actions? Do we have free will? Most of the time we feel in control. But sometimes we don't. In those moments we believe we're justified to say, 'It wasn't my fault'. But why not? Sure, circumstances can make some options more difficult than others. But does that give us an excuse? Should we be held responsible for our actions even if we're stressed, depressed or conditioned by our environment?

Take cheating, for example. If a man cheats on his wife does he have any right to blame his actions on the other woman, peer pressure, or his wife's behaviour? It's not uncommon for a man to explain away his actions. Often men don't want to take responsibility. And, sadly, it's not unusual for the wife to blame herself. But would a man (or woman for that matter) cheat if their partner were in eyeshot of their actions. I think not. So why shouldn't they take responsibility for something they know they shouldn't do?

Every action we take has consequences. But often we take irresponsible action despite being fully aware of the ramifications. For example, we may know buying that dress, computer or car will plunge us into unmanageable debt. But we buy it anyway. In many situations we're at the mercy of our desires. We react to impulses instead of taking the time to consider the consequences. But for a healthier and more fulfilling life we need to learn how to take deliberate and considered action. We need to change reaction into response. In short, we need to take responsibility.

We might not have complete control in life. We may be a slave to convention. But we do have the power to break free of the chains that bind us to a particular pattern of behaviour. What's more, even if the world is a deterministic system we do have some control of how we get to the end point. In other words, we're all going to die – that has been determined for us and we can't control that fact – but we do have control of how we experience the ride. You see, we can always choose our attitude in response to life's events. We can choose to take the high road or the low road.

> *We can always choose our attitude in response to life's events.*

No doubt, habits inhibit your response-ability. They cause you to react. But you can change your limiting patterns of behaviour. You just need to become more aware of them. Take a step back and observe yourself in action. Remember: to change an action you must first become aware of it. And it's in that moment of awareness that you have the opportunity to try something new. It's your chance to respond rather than to react. Respond straight away and your challenges will become opportunities. React, and expect life to stay the same or get worse.

PART TWO

Right Practice

CHAPTER 21

Act

For a long time I've been curious about the difficulties that most of us have when it comes to taking action – the type of action that leads to a healthier and more fulfilling life. We vow to stop smoking, go to the gym or stop bingeing on junk food. We may get motivated for a while and take action for a day or two, but it doesn't last. So how do we maintain our motivation, not just for a couple of days, but for weeks, months or even years?

In a word: emotion. In fact, the word 'emotion' is derived from the Latin *movere* – to move. And therein lies the key to staying motivated. You see, we often know what we want to achieve and the reason why. But this intellectual understanding is not enough to get us going, let alone keep us motivated. With intellectual insight, we say something like: 'Yes, I know what I need to do in my head, but I don't really feel it in my heart'. What we're acknowledging here is our lack of emotional insight.

Take smoking, for example. Most smokers understand the dangers of smoking – they have intellectual insight – but they continue to smoke. But many women who have battled for years to give up smoking find that when they become pregnant they manage to stop – at least for the entire course of their pregnancy. And that's because of the deep compassion they have for their child, and concern for its welfare.

Emotion is a powerful motivator. When you feel passionate about your goals you'll always act on the knowledge, advice and insights that will help you to achieve them. Remember: keep your head and heart going in the right direction and you won't have to worry about your feet.

But if your dream, goal or passion is still not strong enough to get you going, then you may need to search a little deeper. You see, putting off an important activity is often a way to avoid an unpleasant emotional state.

For example, you may put things off because you fear failure. Or maybe you don't like being told what to do. Or perhaps you're afraid of success. Not because you don't value success, but because you're afraid of losing it once you attain it. You look at the top of the mountain and say: 'The view from the top may be great, but it'd be a nasty fall'. Often we're not avoiding a task; we're avoiding an undesirable feeling. But there is a solution.

> *Emotion is the driving force in your life*
> *but it's also the brakes.*

The key to taking action: give it meaning. So if your life is full of clutter, for example, and you're hopelessly disorganised, you need to think about the benefits of blitzing the clear-out. Perhaps you'll feel more settled, liberated and able to focus on other areas of your life. Attach emotion and you'll be far more likely to act. The bottom line: emotion is the driving force in your life but it's also the brakes. So you need to understand the emotions that drive you, and the ones that hold you back.

CHAPTER 22

Change

Life is about growing. If you don't change, you don't grow. If you don't grow, be prepared to feel massive amounts of pain. You see, life wants the best for us. It wants us to be the best we can be. So it guides us with a nudge. But if we ignore the nudge, it whacks us sideways.

Think about it: when do we finally learn about people management? When we lose our key people. When do we start to seek a better work/life balance? When our body or family is falling apart. When do we try to find our true vocation? After we've been passed up for promotion or made redundant. For many, if there's no pain then there's no impetus to change. But life doesn't have to be a series of painful lessons, if we listen to the gentle signals. You see, pain doesn't come suddenly – it increases bit by bit. It guides us with a beam of light. Most people change, however, not because they see the light, but because they feel the heat.

Often people are reluctant to change because it's accompanied with awkwardness and discomfort. You have to give up security for a while. It takes you out of your comfort zone. For some it could mean giving up a familiar but limiting pattern of behaviour, safe but unrewarding work, or a relationship that has lost its meaning. But if you're dynamic, open-minded and flexible you can transform your experience of change. Especially when life is moving in the wrong direction.

But if change is already burning at the seat of your pants, here's the best way to turn down the heat. First, accept your current situation and resist the urge to act impulsively. Now I'm not suggesting you just put up with it. What you need to do is look at it without slipping into habitual reactions. Say: 'Okay, I see you. I know this is a call to change. Now I'm going to take some time to consider the most appropriate response'.

Next, take responsibility for your situation. Of course you're hardly responsible if your roof caves in because of a storm. However, if you don't take responsibility for whatever happens, you're likely to fall into the unhelpful victim mindset. What you need to be asking yourself is: 'How can I grow from this experience?'.

Then, identify what you need to change to deal with the situation. This is where you home in on the lesson you need to learn. Your situation may be teaching you to be more assertive, a more attentive partner or to achieve a balance between life and work.

Finally, take action. For the entire course of your time on this earth you'll be presented with lessons to learn. Every change you make will catapult you further along the path to fulfilment. In every lesson there is an opportunity for a new and better life.

If we are honest, we don't want things to stay the same. Who doesn't want some aspect of their life to improve? Without change there would be no hope of a better life, or

> *The pain of changing now will always be less than the pain of staying the same.*

an end to suffering. Change from bad to good is desirable. But understand: all change is for the better, no matter in what direction it's heading. And remember not to resist change. Because the pain of changing now will always be less than the pain of staying the same. So be proactive – seek change before it finds you!

CHAPTER 23

Compete

There are two schools of thought when it comes to competitive karate. One school believes it brings progress by encouraging the development of skills. The other camp believes it breeds jealousy, greed or envy for another person's position or titles.

Competition is a controversial topic in karate and in life. But no matter where you stand on the issue you can hardly avoid it. You will always find yourself competing for something, whether you've got your eye on a newly created position in your company or that last seat on the train.

I'm all for competition. As I'll explain in a bit, sometimes a competitor can provide more help for your development than a good friend. But when competition is taken too far it becomes an unhealthy and undesirable motivational force.

You see, many competitors hate the people who are better than them because they see them as being in a position to block their progress. They also fear those they view as being just below them because they fear they may somehow get above them. In short, competition leads people to begrudge winners, disrespect losers and to be suspicious of just about everyone.

Think about how much time and energy is wasted watching your back instead of getting on with life. There must be a better way to live than in the tension-filled world of competition. Well, there is a better way and it doesn't mean you have to avoid competition altogether. If you compete with the right attitude it can bring out the best in you.

> *If you compete with the right attitude it can bring out the best in you.*

Understand: there will always be people who are more knowledgeable, more talented or more popular than you are. Don't measure yourself against others. Don't let others dictate what goals you set for yourself. Instead, set goals and targets that make sense to you. Compete with yourself. Measure your growth this year in terms of your progress last year rather than against your opponent's progress.

Time for that explanation I promised earlier.

We all have an inbuilt desire to grow, and growth is best achieved when we're faced with a challenge. Challenges pull us out of our comfort zone. When we are presented with difficulties we dig into the depths of our abilities and realise the true limits of our potential. In karate your opponents do their best to make things difficult for you. By playing the role of your enemies they become your true friends. By competing with you they in fact cooperate with you. Having a worthy opponent is a blessing: it encourages you to be your very best.

So as you make the transition from comparing yourself to improving yourself, from seeing your opponents as enemies to seeing them as friends, remember: life will always provide you with the challenges and worthy opponents that require you to grow.

CHAPTER 24

Compromise

Martial artists ultimately strive for harmony. Sure they train to fight, but paradoxically that gives them a choice not to. They don't back down from conflict, they seek to resolve it. They look for the common ground, areas of agreement. They compromise.

Most people shy away from conflict. They hate to fight. But opposing attitudes, opinions or approaches don't have to turn into a wrestling match. Conflict can be positive. But, still, most people avoid it. And they end up feeling frustrated and resentful towards other people. However, be very clear: inaction doesn't solve disagreements. Conflict needs to be managed before it becomes a destructive force.

A lot can be learnt from the martial arts when it comes to handling conflict. Martial artists understand the importance of taking early action. They're vigilant. They monitor the climate. And their powers of observation give them an early warning system. If they detect conflict in the air, they don't become aggressive or avoid solving the situation. They stay calm and assertive. They take the time to understand the real cause of the situation. They see the other person's point of view. And they find an acceptable way forward. Simply put: they compromise.

Make no mistake: compromise isn't about lowering your standards or giving up your values for others. It's about reducing your demands or changing your opinion in order to reach an agreement. Compromise is wrong when it means sacrificing a principle. We all have standards. And if our minimum level isn't met it's going to lead to disharmony. So strike the right balance. Don't compromise yourself.

> ### *Compromise is wrong when it means sacrificing a principle.*

Conflict can evoke strong emotions so the key is to deal with it when you're feeling calm. Refrain from knee-jerk reactions. Take time to think the problem through and plan a constructive way to handle the situation. Reach an agreement that is acceptable to both sides.

CHAPTER 25

Decide

In life, there is always a choice to make. At every moment of the day we have to decide what to focus on, what to think about and what to do. But often we operate from automatic patterns of behaviour. We jump to conclusions, react impulsively and think repetitive thoughts. But to live a more fulfilling life we need to learn how to make clear, conscious and unbiased decisions.

We've all had the experience of feeling indecisive. It's an uncomfortable feeling. So often, to avoid the discomfort, we make snap decisions, react, and stick to old patterns. To make better decisions, though, we need to accept things being in limbo for a while. We need to take a step back. When we consider the details of our situation and all the available options we can see clearly what needs to be different and the possibilities for change. Simple questions like: 'What exactly is happening now?' and 'How is this a problem for me?' can help to provide that clarity. So when in doubt see it as a signal to stop and think.

Another hindrance to making better decisions is the fear of being wrong. We don't want to make a mistake. So we stay stuck. And instead of creating space to see clearly we create anxiety, and allow things to get worse. Understand: we won't always be able to make the right decision. But we can always make our decision right. In other words, whatever we decide, the outcome of our decision will provide us with a lesson. And if we listen and learn we'll be one step closer to making the right decision.

> *We won't always be able to make*
> *the right decision. But we can always*
> *make our decision right.*

For instance, you may choose the wrong partner or job but at least you'll know that's not what you want. Next time you'll have a better idea of what you're looking for and what's important. So don't hold back. Make the decision. Listen to the feedback. And then make adjustments.

In karate, you have to act boldly when you're sparring. You can never be sure if your choice of attack will be successful. In spite of your doubts you have to step forward courageously and strike. Without full commitment you're likely to get hurt. Act as if it were impossible to fail and you get results. It's the same with major decisions in life. Take your time to assess the situation, and then act confidently as if it were impossible to fail. Simply put: wait long and strike fast.

CHAPTER 26

Defend

For as long as humans have been on this earth we have been a snack for wild beasts, or even other humans. Thousands of years ago when a hungry lion sniffed us out, or a marauding warrior tracked us down, we had one of three choices: run, fight or die. Often running wasn't an option – have you ever tried to outrun a lion? So, really, there were only two choices: fight or die. Clearly dying doesn't take much practice – so we quickly learnt to fight.

Today there's not much chance of a wild beast hunting you down. And, thankfully, unprovoked physical attacks are rare. So there isn't much need for self-defence. But what isn't rare is unprovoked emotional attacks – which, incidentally, can feel like a wild beast hunting you down. The trouble is we have highly developed martial arts but few forms of emotional self-defence. I guess what we need most is training in 'tongue-fu', not kung-fu. So in a bit I'll show you some defensive techniques.

But before I do, let's face it.

Everybody likes to please others. If we please our friends, boss or peers they're more likely to help us. And if we want to keep our jobs and friends it helps if these people think good things about us too. But sometimes we're so eager to be liked we end up working too hard to please others and forget to please ourselves. Other times we take the need to please too far and allow others to manipulate and abuse us.

Unfortunately there'll always be people who for whatever reason dish out abusive jokes, try to manipulate you with emotional blackmail, or sabotage your professional objectives with political behaviour. But you don't have to be a passive victim. Not if you defend yourself. So take a stand. But set limits because you don't want to be on edge or overreact to every ambiguous comment or gesture. If you feel things have been taken too far, first go in with a light tap. If the behaviour doesn't stop, try again. If a tap still doesn't work, don't hesitate … go in with a knockout punch.

> **You don't have to be a passive victim,**
> **take a stand.**

Here's how.

When you feel that another's request or demand would be too stressful for you, say: 'No', not in an abrupt or rude way. Next say the person's name: 'Jess'. Finally, let the person know how you feel, 'Look, I feel awkward saying this but …'. Explain why you must say no: 'I'm worried that if I do this for you I won't be able to get some other important things done'. Put the three steps together and you get something like this: 'Look, Jess, I really find it hard to say no because I don't want to appear inconsiderate, but I've given it a lot of thought and I will have to say no this time. I've got enough on my plate and if I take on more, I won't be able to manage'.

And if you're faced with abusive language then start by pausing. Hold back your emotions for a moment and take a deep breath. It's not easy, but it may defuse the situation. Once the person has vented, play back the gist of their message – without the expletives: 'If I understand you correctly …'. Then, if you have a remedy for the person's issue, put it forward. If not, ask the person: 'How would you like to resolve this?' If the person's solution is unfeasible, negotiate an alternative: 'I can't do that, but here's what I can do'.

The key to self-defence is to be firm but reasonable. Don't avoid conflict. Learn to rock the boat a little. State your opinions. Take a stand.

CHAPTER 27

Focus

On a daily basis we're bombarded with information, opportunities and tasks that compete for our attention. So often we find ourselves trying to do more than one thing at a time – which is actually impossible. Our mind can only focus on one thing but it will jump continuously between each thing. And those things are not always what we want to be focusing on. We tend to start one job and break off intermittently as we remember the other things we should be doing.

There's a lot of stuff that can distract us in life. But to get things done we need the ability to move and sustain our attention. It's amazing how much of our life we waste thinking about the past or worrying about the future. Scattered attention makes us unproductive. If we think and do a lot of things at once, we do none of them well. To do our best work, to achieve our most important goals, we must be fully absorbed in our activities.

Meditation can help you to develop focus. It trains your mind to stay in the present. It's the practice of paying attention to one thing at a time and learning how to sustain that focus. That one thing can be anything – an object, person, sound or feeling – absolutely anything. But what's important is to have only one point of focus. When you're able to focus on the present, you can bring your entire mind to the task at hand, and you'll have developed a key success skill.

> ### *What's important is to have only one point of focus.*

Here's a simple meditation exercise that can help you to develop your ability to focus. Get a sheet of white paper and draw a black dot in the centre. The dot should be about one centimetre in diameter. Next, stick the paper on a wall at eye level. Now, for 1 minute, focus your attention on the black spot. It doesn't matter if you sit or stand but try to keep your back straight, head up and relax.

No doubt you will experience your mind drifting from your point of focus. This is natural, so don't be too hard on yourself. Don't force yourself to concentrate, just gently bring your attention back to the black spot each time your mind wanders. This is the process of meditation. When you are able to focus for 1 minute try 2, then 3, and so on.

Developing focus is like developing a muscle – it takes time and effort. Practise for short periods of time, 5 to 10 minutes, regularly, rather than longer but more infrequent sessions. Setting aside a period of time each day for practice will help you develop the habit.

In sport, focus is what separates the amateurs from the pros. At work, it separates the average performers from the stars. In life, it separates you from where you are now and where you want to be. If you have a short attention span you'll never be able to stick to a pursuit for long enough to be successful at it. You'll always be bouncing from task to task, project to project, interest to interest, always busy but never getting anything of value done.

Your aim should be to perform any activity with precise attention, moment by moment, whenever you want. This isn't easy. It's the nature of the mind to hop from one thing to the next. But with practice you can learn to calm this mental activity – increasing your ability to focus on one thing for an extended period. You'll be more relaxed, you'll be able to think more clearly and you'll see solutions to problems more readily.

CHAPTER 28

Forgive

We all have a threshold for forgiveness. Turn up 5 minutes late to meet some people and, hey, no problem. Turn up fifteen minutes late and they'll be seething with fury. You see, we all have a book of rules for living: what's right and what's wrong, what's acceptable and what's not. And somewhere in the small print is a clause that states: 'All human beings must abide by the rules of this book'. And, if they don't … .

Now this might come as a shock so please brace yourself. Understand: your rulebook is not the only rulebook. In fact, there are probably as many rulebooks as there are humans on this planet. Sure, there's some overlap in themes: 'Thou shalt not kill' and the like. But, when it comes to everyday life it's the small things such as: 'Thou shalt not turn up fifteen minutes late' that matter. In other words, it's the infringement of our subtle, personal rules that leads to resentment.

Following that revelation, if you're not suffering from post-traumatic stress this is guaranteed to take you there. As strange as it might sound humans are designed to make mistakes. That's right. We will always make errors. Let's face it. We disappoint people on a regular basis. Who doesn't? What's more, we will continue to slip up, blunder and miss the mark.

If that weren't the case we'd never evolve. We'd have no motivation to improve. There'd be nothing to improve.

So why do we find it so difficult to forgive people when they break our rules? It's bizarre. We don't resent a duck for quacking because that's what ducks do, but if our best friend, mate or lover fails to adhere to Section 34b of our personal rulebook, that's it. They must pay. Usually the penalty of choice is tit for tat, retaliation or revenge. But is it necessary to lower our behaviour to the kind that we thought was unacceptable in the first place? Other times the penalty is more sophisticated: a boycott of the relationship. In both cases we want whoever hurt us to know how much we hurt, so we punish them. We want them to feel our pain or worse. But when we refuse to forgive we only end up punishing ourselves.

Now if you're still with me after that reasoning, this is likely to finish you off. You see, in a sense, there's no reason to forgive anyone for anything. Because forgiveness implies there is an intention in somebody's mistake. But we're never at our best when we hurt other people. We're always doing the best we can, given where we are, what circumstances we're facing, and the tools we have to deal with those situations. If we really knew better, we'd do better.

You can decide how to take it.

Not easy, I know. We all have our limits. However, be very clear, you give others the power to hurt you. And you can reclaim that power. If someone offends, disrespects or insults you, remember, you can decide how to take it. See the person as being confused, imperfect, emotionally unbalanced, in need of love and attention, in pain or fragile, then you'll find it easier to be compassionate. What's more, there'll be no need to forgive.

This way of living doesn't mean you must let people walk all over you. Defend when you need to defend. But don't keep rehearsing the 'wrong' in your mind, rubbing the salt into the wound over and over. Languishing in mental agony won't make you feel better. And, in the end, this is all about making yourself feel better. More peace of mind and joy is the aim. So don't rub it in, rub it out.

CHAPTER 29

Give

For some, the word 'give' means sacrifice. But there's a big difference between giving and sacrifice. Giving is based on a genuine desire to help others. Sacrifice stems from the myth that in order to provide others with something you have to deprive yourself of it first. The 'provide and deprive' myth runs deep. But giving is for your benefit. It's for your fulfilment. 'Isn't that selfish?' you may ask. Yes, it is. But on a deeper level, you serve your self-interest by helping others. Let me explain.

Giving is healthy. Nature is constantly giving up stuff and renewing itself: a tree sheds its leaves; your body sheds its skin; the sun releases its heat. You see, if things multiply in nature without dying and renewing then the system suffers. It becomes a hindrance to its health and development. When we withhold, collect and cease to let go, we become a hindrance to ourselves. So forget 'provide and deprive' and replace it with 'give to live'.

> *Giving is healthy. Nature is constantly giving up stuff and renewing itself.*

Often when people give, in the back of their minds they're expecting something equally valuable back – maybe not today or tomorrow, but sometime in the future. They give to receive – not from life but directly from the person they gave to. But that's a mistake. There's no need to run a set of accounts for the recipients of your gifts.

Understand: when you give, life will always provide you with what you need. So don't be concerned about what you get back from others. When you have faith in the idea that life will provide you with what you need, you'll feel free to give without expecting something back. You'll give in the same manner that a rose gives you the experience of seeing the colour red or the scent of its perfume. Giving becomes part of your nature. You give for the sheer joy of giving.

In short: give your resources, talents and abilities to make a difference in the lives of others. Be generous. It's the path to a more satisfying life.

CHAPTER 30

Let go

Most human suffering occurs because we don't know how to let go. For example, we hold on to unpleasant thoughts and experiences when we should let them pass. Or we try to solve emotional problems by replaying the episode that triggered the emotion over and over. But in our efforts we end up perpetuating the suffering instead of making things better. What we need to do is learn to let go and allow the bad feelings to dissipate naturally, because eventually they will.

> *Allow the bad feelings to dissipate naturally, because eventually they will.*

It's like riding a stationary bike in a gym. If you stop peddling, the wheels will eventually come to a stop. Holding onto a thought is like adding to the spin. We keep peddling. We go over and over the same thoughts in our head. We get wound up. We're not getting anywhere, but our bodies feel like they've just completed the Tour de France.

You see, often we create our own struggles and slow down our progress in life. There is a story that illustrates the point well. Three men set out on a journey. Each carried two sacks around his neck – one in front and one on his back. Which one of them finished first?

The first man was asked what was in his sacks. 'In this one on my back,' he said, 'I carry all the kind deeds of my friends. In that way they're out of sight and out of mind and I don't have to do anything about them. They're soon forgotten. This sack in front carries all the unkind things people do to me. I pause on my journey every day and take these out to study. It slows me down, but nobody gets away with anything.'

The second man said he kept his own good deeds in his front sack. 'I constantly keep them before me,' he said. 'It gives me pleasure to take them out and air them.' 'The sack on your back seems heavy,' someone remarked. 'What's in it?' 'Merely my little mistakes,' said the second man. 'I always keep them on my back.'

The third man was asked what he kept in his sacks. 'I carry my friends' kind deeds in this front sack,' he said. 'It looks full. It must be heavy,' said an observer. 'No,' said the third man, 'it's big, but not heavy. Far from being a burden, it's like the sails of a ship. It helps me move ahead.' 'I notice the sack behind you has a hole in the bottom,' said the observer. 'It seems empty and of very little use.' 'That's where I put all the evil I hear from others,' said the third man. 'It just falls out and is lost, so I have no weight to hinder me.'

The lesson: don't get dragged down by your unpleasant experiences. Learn to loosen your clutch on unhealthy thoughts. Remember, you can't enjoy today if you're thinking about all the bad things that happened to you yesterday.

CHAPTER 31

Listen

Have you ever noticed: people who talk less tend to say more? It may even be fair to say, people who talk less get paid more. Most of us don't think of listening to be a skill we get paid for, because it's something we do naturally. But we fail to understand the difference between hearing and listening. You see, hearing is involuntary, but listening is voluntary. The old Chinese proverb makes this point well: 'We look but we don't see; we hear but we don't listen …'. To listen we must pay attention.

Your attention is a valuable commodity. Organisations pay vast sums of money to make TV commercials and design posters that grab your attention. There are sounds, songs and jingles that compete for your attention too. But listening is the act of consciously focusing on one of them. It's not a passive activity. It's a choice.

> **Your full attention is the most valuable gift you can give to another.**

In fact, your full attention is the most valuable gift you can give to another. It's an act of love. Pay little attention to your partner and soon your partner will have little attention for you. Pay little attention to your children and soon they'll have little attention for anything. Aka: attention deficit disorder. Your attention affirms the other person's existence. Nobody wants to be ignored or feel like they don't matter. In a sense, love is simply attention.

It's always a compliment to be called a good listener. And you can't fake it. People know when they're not being listened to. When we listen we fully understand the needs of our partners, reduce miscommunications and build strong relationships. Listening is at the heart of communication, and everything that helps you to be a good communicator is valuable in career terms too.

Unfortunately, people who want to climb the career ladder often believe that talking a lot will help them more than listening. And that's because they see that well-rewarded people are often confident, articulate, eloquent, filled with interesting ideas and things to say. But in their efforts to sound smart they use complex language and ambiguous terminology, criticise their colleagues' ideas in meetings and snip the ends off others' sentences. Simply, they talk a lot and don't listen enough.

But listening isn't all about other people. It's about listening to yourself too. You see, if we learn to pause and have periods of silence we can uncover the guide within. We all have an inner guide but we don't always make full use of it. Often, there's too much noise going on in our heads. But you'll find the quieter you become the more you can hear. There's no need to search for the guide. You simply need to become aware of it. The fact is: we all hear, feel, or know the right thing to do but few of us listen.

CHAPTER 32

Pause

In karate, regular practice, repetition and maximum exertion are essential if you want proficiency, but only up to a point. There's nothing to gain from overtraining. Fitness is a product of work and rest. It's during the pauses that the body grows stronger. It's the same with all activities in life. Progress requires regular breaks. In fact, the best thing to get out of exercise is rest … rest and activity; rest and activity; rest and activity. It's like a song chanted by every living thing. It's the soundtrack to life.

> **Rest and activity; rest and activity. It's the soundtrack to life.**

The trouble is, in today's must-get-something-done culture we hardly find time to get sufficient sleep let alone rest. Society doesn't encourage us to take time out and pause. Most of our time is spent chasing things, doing stuff and trying to 'make it'. And we have a lot of criteria for 'making it'. Money, fame, power and status are all measures of success. And most of us strive to meet these criteria. Make no mistake: having goals is important. There's nothing wrong with doing things. But you can slow down. You can take a breather. The wheels of the cart won't fall off.

Pauses are an integral part of sparring in karate. Watch a professional at work and you'll notice attack and defence don't always occur continuously. Good fighters pause to look for openings, observe reactions and revise their strategy. In contrast, novice fighters pile in with a relentless flow of attacks. They soon get exhausted, and often they leave themselves open to danger. It's the same in life: we don't always achieve more by running faster or trying harder. Sometimes it's more productive to take a step back and pause.

Ever felt stuck in life? You know the feeling. You're trying everything to move forwards but it's as if you're spinning your wheels, nothing seems to work. Most of us (me included) have had this experience. And the best thing to do when you have tried everything and nothing seems to work is ... nothing. Pause. Remain still and the right action will arise by itself. The 1973 film classic *Enter the Dragon* portrayed this approach well when Bruce Lee found himself trapped in a lift, not knowing what to do next. He sat down. Crossed his legs. And paused. Then after a short while his escape route appeared. Sometimes we just need to accept the current situation and see what comes up. Action that arises out of this foundation works. In stillness there's clarity.

Slowing down isn't just about the movement of the body, though, it's also about the movement of the mind. You see, even when the body is resting the mind can still be rushing. When you rush it's as if your mind leaps out of your head (if that's where it lives). But when you pause mentally, you get it back. Even when you're relaxing on your sofa, if your mind isn't at rest, nor are you. Mental rushing is like running on the spot, you're not getting anywhere, but you still feel exhausted.

To rest mentally stay focused in the moment. Stop replaying events from the past or thinking about how things might be in the future. Acknowledge where you are right now and what is happening. Take a break. Slow down. Pause.

CHAPTER 33

Plan

Now I'm sure you don't need me to bang on about why we should plan. We've all heard the old saying: 'If you don't plan, you plan to fail'. In fact, it'd be difficult to find a personal development book that doesn't mention the importance of planning. It's like a mantra repeated over and over, and over … and over. It puts you to sleep. But now is the time to wake up to the wisdom locked in that message. Everyone is saying the same thing for a reason – planning works.

When you have a dream you'll be able to generate the passion and commitment needed to get the results you desire. But a dream with no plan is useless. Understand: it does no harm to dream, providing you get up and put your plan to work when the alarm goes off. This is your wake-up call.

Converting your dream into a series of manageable action steps and putting deadlines to them takes the 'wish' element out of it. In fact, a plan is simply a dream or goal with a deadline. Look at it this way. Imagine that a relative is getting married in a city that is 300km from your home. The ceremony starts at nine in the morning. This is your goal: to arrive at your relative's wedding for 9am. Now you need to plan how you're going to achieve it.

> *A plan is simply a dream or goal with a deadline.*

If you decide to drive, that might mean leaving your house at 6am, which would give you three hours to complete the journey. Before you set out, it'd be prudent to look at a map and get an idea of where you're heading. You never know, if you explore different routes you may find a shortcut. Plus, it'd be sensible to check if there are any roadworks that might delay your journey too. It's the same in life. If you plan you might discover shortcuts and take roads with as little obstruction as possible.

Next, you need to think about the steps you'll take to achieve your goal. How fast will you have to drive? Will you take any breaks? How much fuel will you need? Does your car require a service? These are just some of the things you might need to consider to reach your destination according to schedule. Be very clear: it's the detail that has the power to move your plan to your muscles. So think things through carefully before acting.

And don't forget, plans need to be flexible too. Take DJs, for example. They prepare playlists for each party. But they can change the list, or order of songs, depending on how the crowd reacts to the music. You see, as you put your plan into action there will be times when you have to make adjustments. Plans aren't static. They should be altered and updated to meet new circumstances. In this world all things change, life is change. And so be prepared to change your plans too.

Understand: things don't always work to plan. But setting a direction for where you are going in life, or any other significant goal, is better than sitting back and hoping for the best. You can't leave everything to the motion of the ocean. There's no guarantee the tide will land you on the shore of your choice.

CHAPTER 34

Play

Some people seem to take this whole self-development business too seriously. Perhaps that's because, for some, 'making it' or winning is all that matters in life. Give it a break, I say. But other people don't take themselves seriously enough. For them, the only thing that matters is having fun. Wise up, is my advice. You see, we need to aim for the middle ground, because a more fulfilling life requires a balance between playfulness and seriousness. Yes, that b word again.

> *The number one deathbed regret is taking life too seriously. So don't let it be yours.*

In our must-get-something-done culture there is often little time to play and have fun. But know this now: the number one deathbed regret is taking life too seriously. So don't let it be yours. What's more, having fun will keep you away from that bed for longer, because play and laughter is good for your health. It helps to reduce stress and it releases endorphins that give you a natural high.

Understand: having fun doesn't have to involve crazy, reckless behaviour. Fun in life means more smiling, more laughter and better relationships. It has benefits at work too. And, as I've discovered in karate, it's a performance enhancer. Chuang Tzu, the Chinese philosopher, put it well when he said: 'When archers shoot for enjoyment, they have all their skills; when they shoot for a brass buckle, they get nervous; when they shoot for a prize of gold, they begin to see two targets'. You see, when you're relaxed, playful and not fixed on the outcome performance improves.

Sadly, having fun isn't acceptable in all environments. Early on in my career my manager told me I wouldn't be taken seriously if I smiled too much. I'm not kidding. Some people truly believe they must become serious to be taken seriously. I disagree. It shows confidence, control and authority if you can lighten the atmosphere. What's more, if you're having fun at work you'll be less stressed, more tolerant of menial tasks and more satisfied with your job. It's not hard work if you're having fun – it's play.

No one is saying we should be all smiles and giggles. That would be inappropriate in most situations. But pick your moments, relax and have fun. It'll help to keep your personal problems in perspective too. Because if you can laugh at your troubles, you'll always have something to laugh at.

CHAPTER 35

Question

Einstein once said that if he were about to be killed and he had only 1 hour to figure out how to save his life, he'd spend the first fifty-five minutes searching for the right question. Then, he believed, it would take less than five minutes to figure out the answer.

Of course, it's unlikely we will ever face such a situation in life. Einstein was simply making a point about the power of questions. But whether we have five, five hundred or five million minutes to live there's a question we could all ask, which has the potential to transform our lives. I'll get to that big question soon, but before I do, let me say this.

As children we have a natural curiosity and we ask questions without restrictions. We want to know why things happen. Why we have to do things a certain way. And, why we need to do them at all. We just keep on asking questions. That's until our natural curiosity is replaced by formal instruction: 'just do as you're told', and 'stop asking questions'.

As adults we still have a natural curiosity but we ask questions less freely. We want to know 'Why?' but we don't want to appear stupid, so we don't ask. But even if we haven't been inflicted with the censure of an oppressive schoolteacher, parent, or critical peers the questions we ask are often the wrong ones. No surprise really – asking questions is a skill and we're rarely given the opportunity to develop it. So here's a crash course.

Top tip: don't ask information-gathering questions; ask wisdom-activation questions. You see, each information-gathering question leads to another question. Perhaps that's the reason why parents become impatient with children who incessantly ask: 'Mum, why this …'. 'Dad, why that …'. 'But, why …'. There's no end to it. Each answer leads to another question. Now I'm not suggesting you give up learning. There's nothing wrong with a bit of knowledge. But life isn't a school of knowledge; it's a school of wisdom.

> *Life isn't a school of knowledge; it's a school of wisdom.*

It's as if we become addicted to the satisfaction of knowing. But that knowing doesn't last for long. We may know about the why of this, but what about the why of that? Fast-forward and we're left with the why of the world. In the end, we get stuck. When we ask wisdom-activation questions, however, we move forward. As you'll see shortly, wisdom-activation questions lead to solutions. Information-gathering questions lead nowhere.

When you take this learning and apply it to Einstein's conundrum you see how it could literally save your life. Think about it. If you had one hour to save your life, there'd be no point asking 'Why me?' 'Why is this happening?' You'd waste your time. You'd be better off asking wisdom-activation questions: 'What do I need to get through this?' 'What will get me what I want?' 'What will I do?' And if you still couldn't find an answer to save yourself, then you could always ask: 'Who do I choose to be in the face of death?'

And so. There we have it. As promised, the big question: 'Who do I choose to be?' The point: no matter what challenges, hardships or circumstances you face in life you can always choose your attitude. A shift in attitude has the potential to move any problem to a solution. It can move you from feeling stuck to living in possibility. In fact, it's less of a question to answer and more of a guide for living.

CHAPTER 36

Relax

Relaxation allows us to recharge, stay calm and make full use of our energy. When we relax, it's like the kinks being loosened out of a hose. Our energy can flow freely, without obstruction. And as the energy surges through our body we regain the natural drive to take action.

To be at our best, however, we need a balance of tension and relaxation. Imagine what would happen if you lost the ability to tense the muscles in your body. You'd collapse in a heap. Tension is an important part of life. We need it to do most things. But living with unnecessary tension is like trying to drive a car with the handbrake half on. To move forward at an unrestricted speed we need to release the brakes.

Most of us have become used to living with unnecessary tension in our bodies. Shoulders are often the most common place to find it. They're the place where we have traditionally been thought to carry the burdens of life. Remind yourself to drop your shoulders and you'll be surprised how often there is something to drop.

Unnecessary tension saps our energy like a water leak dripping down a drain. And if it continues, in time it can lead to physical illness. To reverse this process we need to learn to relax. How? Start with the body. The body is the way in and the way out.

> *Unnecessary tension saps our energy*
> *like a water leak dripping down*
> *a drain.*

Much of the tension in your body isn't noticeable because your mind is usually focused outwards. But to relax your body you need to become aware of it. So turn your focus inwards. What is your posture like right now? Are you slumped on a sofa or slouching in a chair? Are you comfortable? Is your posture creating tension somewhere in your body? Remember, if your body is tight it's wasting energy. If you become aware of the tension and just stay with the sensations you'll naturally adjust your posture. And, eventually, you'll feel the hardness dissolve.

Relaxing the body is one thing, but learning to relax the mind is just as important. In fact, tension in the mind creates tension in the body. Think negative, unhealthy, bitter thoughts and immediately you'll notice a contraction in your muscles. Understand: hurtful thoughts hurt the body. Learn to relax the mind and you'll learn how to let go of unhealthy thoughts. You'll be on your way to a more energetic life.

So how do we relax the mind? Conscious breathing is the key. We're not normally aware of our breathing, and that's because in most situations we do it without thinking. It's only when we have our breath taken away from us that we become aware of it. And when we lose it we quite literally lose our mind. You see, your brain relies on oxygen to survive. Cut off the oxygen supply and it stops functioning.

But when we focus on our breath we naturally regain our ability to breathe well. So, sit up. Relax and notice your breath entering and leaving your body. Don't try to breathe, just let it happen. When your mind wanders gently bring it back to your breath. That's the way to relax your mind. It's the way to reclaim your full mental faculties. When we keep the mind on the breath we bring it to the present moment. We release ourselves from compulsive thoughts. What's more, we feel better and function better.

CHAPTER 37

Simplify

Mastering karate techniques is about getting the greatest possible return on any energy you expend. Skilful fighters make no unnecessary moves. They simplify their techniques so that they're executed with the utmost efficiency. Their hands don't wind up before they strike. They take the shortest path to the target. They understand the simple punch is the most powerful punch. So they avoid the use of complex techniques. In short: they keep it simple.

The life parallel: often we make so many unnecessary moves in life. We chase the bigger house, faster car or bigger boat. We always want more. More money. More fame. More gadgets. More shoes. And we end up having to do more to get more. Ultimately, our cravings and desires lead to a more complicated life. We pursue *wants* instead of *needs*. We try to keep up with the neighbours and end up working longer hours, getting extra jobs and feeling more stressed.

The solution: reduce your *wants* and your life will be simplified. The best way to achieve this is to make a list of all the things you need and then hack away at the inessentials – the *wants*. You have to be very clear about this because *wants* often creep on to your list and mask themselves as necessities. You see, the mind has a tendency to justify the things you don't really need in life. If you have trouble eliminating an item, ask yourself: 'Will this provide temporary gratification or lasting fulfilment?' If it's not fulfilling, then it's not a *need*. In other words: if it's not going to fill you up, give it up.

> ***If it's not going to fill you up, give it up.***

Take action: simplify your life. Make it less complex. Prioritise the things you have to do. Work on one task at a time. Don't start anything unless you can finish it. Give certain things up. Remember who and what is most important in your life, and forget the rest. Follow your heart. Learn to say 'no'. Be assertive. Think straight. Talk straight. Say a lot in a few words. And, remember, the simpler you live, the richer life will be. That's 'simplify' in a nutshell.

CHAPTER 38

Stretch

Development comes when you reach out and stretch yourself. It's a product of moving to the edge of your comfort zone and taking yourself a little beyond the point of resistance. It's about facing and overcoming challenges. When you reach for new heights and develop new skills you're more likely to feel satisfied with life. But don't stretch your limits to the point of pain. Discomfort? Yes. Pain? No. In other words, forget: no pain, no gain. And remember: no discomfort, no development.

In karate, a lot of the combinations and drills wouldn't be much practical use in a real fight. But they act as limit-pushing exercises that develop flexibility, strength, balance and coordination – all the stuff that would be useful in combat. You see, when we train in this way we learn to tolerate discomfort. And we develop the will to move into it. It's the only way to improve. It's the same in life. It's at the edge of your comfort zone that you find the next level in your development. So if anything makes you feel uncomfortable, take a close look at it. It's your gateway to a more satisfying life.

Understand: we all need to experience discomfort to develop, so set challenging goals. There's not much fun playing a game you can easily win. When you have to stretch to succeed you get a sense of satisfaction from the achievement. So set targets that take you out of your comfort zone. Reach for new heights. Develop new skills. It'll make you feel more alive and fulfilled.

There is a tendency for all of us to stay comfortable, both physically and mentally. But when we're comfortable we become stiff. We resist change. We learn nothing new, and we don't grow. So stretch every day both physically and mentally. Do something that makes you feel uncomfortable.

> *When we're comfortable we become stiff. We resist change. We learn nothing new, and we don't grow.*

Try this: stand next to a wall, keep your feet flat on the ground, and with a straight arm see how far you can stretch upwards. Now once you get to your limit go for an extra one per cent. See if you can stretch a little further. Most people can. We always have a little extra we can give even when we're at the edge of our limits.

CHAPTER 39

Trust

Imagine that I were to ask you to perform a simple game of trust. Stand in front of me with your back towards me. I will make sure there is a 1-metre gap between us. Now fall back keeping your body straight. Don't look around because I'm going to catch you. Would you trust me? Your answer would be determined by a number of factors. Perhaps the first thing you would want to know is whether I could manage your weight. Then maybe you would like to see me demonstrate my ability with someone else. No doubt, a consistent record of successful catches would lower your fear and perception of risk.

However, my performance and track record are not the only factors that would determine how much you could trust me. You see, we all have our own personal history when it comes to trusting people. A background full of trustful experiences could make it easier for you to trust. Conversely, a background of betrayed trust could leave you highly sceptical of anyone, no matter what you know about them. Neither position is any better than the other. Both can lead to good and bad outcomes. For example, too much trust can lead to careless decisions, whereas an experience of broken trust can make you less gullible and susceptible to having the wool pulled over your eyes.

Unfortunately, there's no universal formula to assess trustworthiness. Sure, it makes sense to observe a person's actions over a period of time before you trust them. But we can never be totally certain of their future actions. So there comes a point when you have to trust your own judgment. You see, at bottom, trust comes back to you. People can never force you to trust them. You must decide to give it. In a sense, trust is exactly that, a gift.

> *There comes a point when you have to trust your own judgment.*

Relationships are built on trust. But that doesn't mean we have to trust a person in every domain before we can forge a bond with them. Trust is not an all or nothing concept. So if you're looking to rebuild trust in a person, remember there's always something you can find to trust about them. People will always demonstrate a consistency in some area of their life – even if that's in the fact that their words and actions are always inconsistent. That may sound strange. But once you know what to expect from a person, good or bad, you'll be in a much better position to rebuild trust.

CHAPTER 40

Win

For some people everything is a contest. They always try to be first, get to the top, or be number one. They compete to have whatever the latest thing is. At work they constantly push for progress, and operate like warriors engaged in battle against the enemy.

Make no mistake. There's nothing wrong with trying to be the best, win, or be number one. In fact, the will to win is an important source of motivation. It provides drive and determination. But to win in life, it pays to remember that 'b' word again: balance.

You see, if winning is the only reason you take part in an activity then you're looking for trouble. When your life is all about one thing, that one thing can break you. So take a step back. Look at the bigger picture. Seek balance. As any professional athlete will tell you: winning does matter, but it's not everything.

True enough, losing isn't easy – especially when you're emotionally attached to the outcome. Winning feels better, for sure. In fact, for most people their self-worth is wrapped up in winning, and that wrapping is easily unravelled. There is, however, an alternative approach to winning. It's a tried and tested approach. An approach that protects you from the dangers that lie on the path to being the best.

So what is it? In short: treat winning and losing the same. Why? Because sooner or later the thrill of winning will subside. And before long you'll have to start working to win again. You see, in the end the outcome is the same. If you lose, you have to work. If you win, you have to work too. That's not to say you shouldn't enjoy your wins. But the jubilation of winning is transitory, and so is the disappointment of losing. The sooner you allow those feelings to pass, the sooner you can get back to the process. Which, in the end, is the real goal.

That's right. In the end, winning is about the process not the product. Put another way: to win, you need to let go of winning. Now that might sound like 'Confusionism' rather than Confucianism, the Chinese philosophy from which the idea originates. But it makes complete sense. As I've learnt in karate, as soon as you start focusing on the goal, you stop listening to the body. You lose the mind-body connection, which is essential for excellence. It's the same in life: focusing on the prize attaches you to the result. Whereas focusing on the process let's you tap your potential, and increase your fun.

> *The best approach to winning is an attitude of detached determination.*

The bottom line: the best approach to winning is an attitude of detached determination. But, remember, the journey is more important than the prize. So try your best. Learn from your mistakes. And enjoy the process. That's the path to winning.

PART THREE

Right Understanding

CHAPTER 41

Awareness

If knowing yourself is the beginning of all wisdom, then know this: there is no self. I kid you not. The concept of the self is an illusion. Now I know that might be hard to swallow in one big chunk so I'm going to break it down into manageable pieces. Perhaps then you might be able to save yourself a bit of money on that trip around the world (or to the top of that mountain) in search of yourself.

So here we go. First, let me be clear: there is no self, but that doesn't mean you're not real (obviously). What it does mean, however, is there is no constant self. No fixed, unchanging, permanent you.

Think about it for a minute. How do you describe yourself? You describe how you look: 'I'm tall with dark hair'. You describe what you do: 'I'm a marathon runner'. You describe what you think: 'I believe external events cause most human misery'. And you describe what you feel: 'I feel anxious about anything that is unknown, uncertain, or potentially dangerous'. Do you see? Not one of these things is permanent. Sure, some of them may stick around a lot longer than the others. They may even repeat themselves. But, to varying degrees, they're all changing. Simply put: you're a process, not a product.

Part two. Now that hopefully I've loosened the roots on the notion of a fixed, constant, permanent self, let me get back to the topic of this chapter: awareness. You see, there is another important aspect of ourselves but, no matter how hard we try, this one can't be described fully. It's the unchanging process of awareness.

Awareness is what makes us conscious of our surroundings and experience. Without it there would be no world. It's a permanent part of us. So if you have visibly aged over the past 10 years but still feel like you're the same person, then perhaps it's because your awareness, the lens through which you view the world, hasn't changed. In a sense, awareness is who you are at the most fundamental level. We can't see awareness in the same way we can't see our own eyes. Awareness is the seer. We can't ever locate it. It doesn't leave a mark. It's not a thing. But in a sense, it's everything.

> ### Awareness is who you are at the most fundamental level.

Now I don't want to lose you with my philosophical musing so let me get back on track. Part three. The point here is we rarely operate from the perspective of pure awareness. We often put layers on top of what we experience. And those layers are made up of our natural tendency to hear what we want to hear and see what we want to see. So we create stereotypes, compromise our relationships and make poor decisions based on inaccurate information. That's the problem.

preferences happen we need to be willing to accept that and live on. This isn't about giving up hope for a better future. It's about making the best of what we get. Sure, we might not be able to control the external world, but we can always choose our attitude in the face of it.

But we don't stop there. We try to control people too. We want to keep them under our thumb so that they won't hurt us. So we check our partner's phone, snoop around and smother them so they won't have a chance to be unfaithful. We know our behaviour isn't right, but we desperately want to avoid emotional pain. However, we fail to understand that, just as it's not possible to control the world, it's not possible to control other people.

In fact, there aren't many things you can control in life, but you can always take control of yourself. There's a danger you'll overlook this point so I'm going to say it again another way: no matter what comes your way you can always decide how to *be* in the face of it. So if you lost your job, would you choose to feel demoralised, battered, hard done by, or would you choose to feel excited about starting a new career? There's always more than one attitude you can take.

> *You can always take control of yourself.*

To sum up: life will not always go our way. And when it doesn't, we need to let it go where it's going because it's probably taking us where we need to be. What's more, if we're honest, we don't always make the right decisions. We don't always know what is best for us. So perhaps it's a blessing that we don't have total control. Just imagine if we did – we'd probably increase our troubles tenfold.

So don't constantly fight life. Pick your battles. When things are out of your control, save your energy. Accept what you're being offered without holding on to your preferences. If you can't control it, go with it. That's the way to transform life.

CHAPTER 43

Ease

Before we even set foot on this Earth, we enter into a contract that binds us to making an effort. No wonder babies cry when they first arrive. In this world there's no free milk. If you want dinner, you'd better make that very clear. And things don't get any better for us adults. To make life work we have to make a bigger effort still.

But most of us want an easy life. We want the fruits without the labour. So we play the lottery, gamble and take chances in the hope of striking it rich. Then, if we're lucky, we can have it all without the hard work. But an easy life doesn't come without effort. Even lottery winners discover their riches won't stop the weeds from growing in their garden or their shoes from getting scuffed. It takes work to maintain material things and everything eventually wears out. Nothing lasts for ever – not even a £10 million jackpot.

But we never seem to get over wanting something for nothing. We yearn for it all, the effortless way. So things fall apart, life gets difficult. Not surprisingly, striving to get something for nothing makes it harder to get what we really want.

What's more, most of us seem to confuse effort with struggle. Effort is putting energy into an activity. Struggle is effort laced with striving and desperation. Perhaps the confusion is a hangover from childhood when we were often told to make an effort. Put in more effort. And try harder. You see, as children, we weren't always clear about what action we needed to take or where to put in the work. And so, when we made a greater effort and the results didn't follow, we became frustrated, tensed up and tried harder still. Soon making an effort became synonymous with struggle.

I see this conditioning at work with adults when they practise karate. Ask them to try harder and they automatically tense their body, which interferes with their performance. They become heavy and have to work against muscles that hold back the ones they need to use. In short: more effort leads to less progress. They end up feeling exhausted when they should be feeling refreshed. It's the same in life: the tension in people's minds and bodies leads to unnecessary struggles and an aversion to making an effort. The best approach: relax into effort. You'll be more responsive to moments when a big push is needed and sensitive to times when it's not.

More effort leads to less progress.

And here's another important point.

To achieve anything worthwhile in life you need to work for it. But be careful not to become too attached to the end result. Life becomes arduous if you cling to outcomes or always want it to be something other than it already is. For an easier life, what you need to do is balance your desire to change with an acceptance of things as they are, right now. Sure, make an effort to improve your life but get yourself in the right state first. When you accept your current situation, and who you are as a person right now, you'll be in the best frame of mind to make improvements. Understand: if your efforts are made from this perspective, you can relax into your pursuits. And there'll be no struggle.

CHAPTER 44

Energy

Energy determines our capacity for action in the world. We use it for everything we do, from reading a book to cooking dinner to making love. Clearly, the more energised we feel, the more fully we can live. But how can we increase our energy levels?

Good healthy nutrition and the air we breathe are our main sources of energy. Essentially, food combines with oxygen to provide us with fuel. However, just like a car that combines petrol with air to power the engine, the food-air combination produces damaging exhaust fumes (or, more technically speaking, free radicals). I'll explain all of this in a bit, but, before I do, understand this.

Humans are built for survival. But, interestingly, the survival of the species is more important than your individual existence. In other words, given the choice between reproduction and repair, your body would choose to make babies. It's as if we're martyrs to the cause of human existence, sacrificing all for the good of the species. But, hey, at least we get to have fun along the way. In any case, the main point here is we can't control the body's energy allocation. But we can control the demand we put on the maintenance and repair function. So if we want more energy, that's the place to look.

So back to free radicals.

When food combines with oxygen in the body to produce energy the by-product is a number of destructive substances called free radicals. But your body has a great defence system to eliminate them: it produces antioxidants to kill them off. But if your system becomes overloaded with the bad stuff, the body looks elsewhere for help. It relies on the nutrients in food. The trouble is the average diet lacks the nutrients that can help: antioxidants. So the body gets damaged, quickly ages, and wastes energy eliminating junk.

In fact, for most people a major energy drain is the body's attempt to extract artificial ingredients from whatever nutrients it can find. It quite literally has to separate the wheat from the chaff. And often that effort is excessive because there's more chaff than wheat. So instead of energising us, the food we eat makes us feel awful. This then triggers a vicious cycle because the body presses us to eat more to get the nutrients it so badly needs. But most people just end up consuming more processed food. And as opposed to feeling fit and fired up, they feel fat and fatigued.

> *Want to feel more energised? Then*
> *start with your diet.*

Want to feel more energised? Then start with your diet. Eat nutrient-rich, unprocessed, plant-based foods. Generally speaking, darker coloured fruit and veg have higher levels of antioxidants. For example: red grapes, blueberries, broccoli and spinach are all high in antioxidants. So start to include some of this good stuff in your diet today.

All that said, increasing energy levels isn't all about nutrition. There are other things that tax the body's maintenance and repair function. For example, overtraining can generate free radicals. So exercise more but in moderate amounts. Excessive tension and negative thinking wastes energy too. So practise relaxation exercises and think less troubling thoughts.

To sum up: if you want to feel and function better you need to give the body's maintenance and repair system less work. So exercise, eat foods and think thoughts that promote energy and health rather than fatigue and premature ageing.

CHAPTER 45

Faith

The bottom line up front: faith is about trust. For example, if I jump out of a plane I put my faith in the parachute on my back. Then I trust that it will open when I pull the string. Although I can't be absolutely certain that it will open until I try it at 3,000 feet. It's the same in life. I believe life wants us to grow. And my faith in the developmental process of life is like my faith in the parachute opening. There's no concrete evidence that life is trying to develop me, or that it will always have my best interests at heart, but my faith in that notion keeps me moving, growing and improving.

In other words, this is my attitude: no matter what happens to me it will always be the best thing for me in the end. You see, karate has taught me you've got to play to win, even if you think the odds are not in your favour. This mindset will always increase your chances of success. Because if you believe life is against you, when the going gets tough you might not have the motivation to improve it. So believe things will work out in the end. This is a healthy perspective. It not only gets you started it also keeps you moving, especially when you face major obstacles. Remember: a believer is an achiever.

But don't get me wrong. I'm not peddling blind faith. Faith isn't hope. It's not about expecting miracles: unaided flying humans or something equally as unlikely. Faith is active. So, of course, inspect your parachute before you take off. There's no point living recklessly. But once you've completed your checks, done all you can to ensure a safe landing, then put your faith in the parachute: the developmental process of life.

Understand: faith is most important when we're dealing with high levels of uncertainty. And that includes any significant life goal. But to live a better, more fulfilling life we need to be comfortable with the unknown. We need to trust whatever each moment brings. We need faith in the perfection of life. Here and now, life is the way it is because that's the way it needs to be. Whatever *is*, is right. Any situation we find ourselves in is ideal for us. This is helpful thinking. But if you adopt this perspective, be fully aware: life will not always appear to be looking out for you. When things get really tough, instead of supporting you life may appear to be punishing you as if you're doing something wrong.

> **Faith is most important when we're dealing with high levels of uncertainty.**

But never forget: we're not here to be punished; we're here to be developed. Just as a wise karate master knows when to strike and how much to throw at students, life provides you with the right amount of challenges that require you to keep coming back to what is best within you. So if you're not winning, improving or getting what you want in life, look for the lesson and have faith you can find it.

CHAPTER 46

Freedom

Life on this planet is full of restrictions. Physical laws govern our everyday actions, they restrict our movements and they define the way we live. But the possibilities within those physical restrictions are endless. Think of it this way: the keys on a piano restrict pianists; however, the music they can create is limitless. So would it really make sense for them to wish for a longer keyboard, more arms, or extra fingers? Do they really need to break free of the restrictions when they can do so much within them? Life's the same: we try so hard to escape when all the freedom we need is within.

For many of us freedom is the licence to do what we want, when we want – without repercussions. For example, we want the freedom to turn up for work at any time. We want the freedom to say what we please, when we please. We want the freedom to smoke or toke. But is that what being free is really about? Not at all. True freedom comes from within. An external authority doesn't grant it. What really matters is freedom from mental habits: impulses, unhealthy thinking and the drive of habitual behaviour.

You see, a desire for freedom is often a desire to be free of pain. Look closely at your vices, bad habits or addictions and you'll notice they are all attempts to avoid unpleasant feelings. We think if we live life freely, going after any pleasant experience, any excitement, perhaps we won't have to feel pain. And we fear a lack of freedom because it might restrict our ability to pursue pleasure and avoid discomfort. We're all looking for freedom from suffering. But most of us are looking in the wrong places. Paradoxically, it's in the discomfort that we find true freedom. In other words, if we want freedom from pain we need to learn how to face it. We need to look inward not outward.

> ## A desire for freedom is often a desire to be free of pain.

It's a bumpy road. Life has many ups and downs. And it's human nature to want to control the lows. In fact most of our life is geared towards managing the dips, and the discomfort that comes with them. But trying to control pain is like trying to stop the tide of an ocean with your hands. You can't hold it back, but you can learn to ride the waves.

We are all limited. We're limited emotionally and physically. And in a sense we are limited in our ability to experience pleasure. Frankly, we weren't built to be free of pain in the same way we weren't built to have more than two arms. So we need to accept pain will always be a part of life and learn to manage it. With this perspective you're less likely to be a slave to your solution. And more likely to feel true freedom.

CHAPTER 47

Goals

We all set goals. Think about it: if you need to catch a train at 8am you get to the station a couple of minutes before. You may run late and miss the train, but you'd only do that a few times before you got tired of missing it. You'd soon get yourself organised to leave earlier, or aim to catch a later train. That's goal setting.

We couldn't survive for long without setting goals. Goals are what keep us going. How often do we hear of someone retiring at sixty and dropping dead within a few months? When we have no purpose in life, no dream or goals, that's it, game over.

The problem with goals is people get caught up in the product, the end result or outcome, when their focus should be on the process. I'm reminded of the story of a student who approaches his karate master and asks, 'How long will it take me to attain a black belt?'. The master replies, 'Five years.'. So the student asks, 'What if I train three days a week?'. 'Ten years,' replies the master. The student asks again, 'What if I train six days a week?'. This time the master answers, 'Fifteen years.'

The point: focus on accomplishing your goal in the present. Do what it takes lesson by lesson and eventually you will get the belt. Make no mistake: it's okay to look at the past and learn from it, picture the future and make plans for it. But to improve the present you must always return to … you guessed it – the present.

But wait. That's not it. You need to be aware of another inherent danger in goal setting. Let me explain. We set goals to close a gap. The gap between the way things are and the way we think they should be. The problem with this approach is we tend to focus on the gap, especially when we face major obstacles, which makes us feel unhappy. Our feeling of discontent saps our motivation and takes us further away from our goal.

You see, for most people, happiness is a by-product of achievement. The trouble occurs when you eventually work out you can't always manipulate or control life. You can't always make things happen. You won't always achieve what you want, when you want. This is when unhappiness strikes. At these times, if you focus on the gap by comparing where you are with where you want to be, you'll increase the gap and your sadness.

> ***It's not what you get from achieving your goals that matters. It's what you become.***

So what can you do? Karate offers an alternative approach to goal setting. It teaches you to treat goals as something simply to aim at. It teaches you to accept goals may not always be reached. And, more importantly, it teaches: it's not what you get from achieving your goals that matters. It's what you become.

CHAPTER 48

Health

They say the body is a temple. Nonsense. It's a bloody miracle. Tell me: where on earth can you find a machine that can digest food and transform the nutrients into energy, circulate fluids to nourish and cleanse, reproduce and recreate, then call itself a temple?

When you think about what the body can do, it's astonishing. And, perhaps, the greatest of all its feats is its ability to clean and heal itself. Sure, we have cars that convert fuel into energy, circulate water to cool and cleanse. But where can you find a machine that has a system to patch up its own scratched bodywork?

Most of us take the body's ability to heal and clean itself for granted. Often it works so well we don't think twice about it. But like any other machine it suffers from wear and tear, and needs constant maintenance. The strange thing is we pay more attention to the machines we own than our bodies. For example: we feed our cars with premium fuel and protective oil. But then we binge on gourmet junk.

OK, to be fair, we get that the health of our teeth is maintained through daily action. But most of us seem to separate our teeth from our bodies (and I'm not talking about wearing dentures). We assume the rest of our body is different. We think its health is in a permanent state. When in fact, just like our teeth, it's in a deteriorating state – unless we take daily action.

So here's what you need to do and why:

1 *Get proper sleep.* That means the right quantity: eight to nine hours. And the right quality: deep, relaxed sleep. Understand: during sleep your body is healing and cleaning itself. It clears the toxins that have accumulated throughout the day. And this happens during different stages of sleep. So if you don't leave enough time for this process, you'll be left with a dirty body. Allow the process to take its full course and you'll wake up feeling refreshed. What's more, you'll greet the day with a grin not a grimace. Remember: your day goes the way the corners of your mouth turn. So get proper sleep.

2 *Eat proper food.* Food provides the body with fuel to function. Eat poor food and expect poor functioning. Continue to eat poor food over a number of years and expect something worse – mal-functioning. So for better health eat lean protein, complex carbohydrates and fresh vegetables. Proper eating is that simple. Of course, simple doesn't mean easy. But with commitment and discipline it *is* possible. So gradually wean yourself off processed, synthetic crap. And when you shop for food, make this your motto: shorter shelf life, longer youthful life.

3 *Get proper exercise.* Most people believe getting and staying in the shape necessary to maximise health takes a lot of time, pain and effort. But staying healthy is more a question

of sensible choices, not brute work or overexertion. The old motto 'no pain, no gain' might hold if you're trying to complete an iron man, but it's not necessarily true when it comes to promoting health. And, remember, you're designed to move not sit on your bottom all day. So if you're able to move, move. Raise your heart rate for at least 20 minutes three times a week. Put bluntly: exercise or expect to expire early.

> *You can't control the length of your life, but you can add life to your years.*

Clearly, you're not going to live for ever. You can't control the length of your life, but you can add life to your years. In other words: it is possible to stay younger for longer. And the only way to do that is sleep well, eat sensibly and work out … or lie about your age.

CHAPTER 49

Joy

Still searching? Will this be it – the final piece in the puzzle, the answer or secret that will put an end to the search? Most of our life is spent searching. And when we're not searching we're chasing or avoiding; constantly doing stuff to find what most of us are looking for – sustainable happiness.

But we fail to understand that all this doing – searching, chasing and avoiding – is actually taking us further away from where we want to be. So we keep on striving for the impossible goal of sustainable happiness. In the process, we take our eye off what really matters, we get distracted and life slips on by. But we don't see the trap. Why? I suppose because it has never been explained to us. Sure, we've all heard that material things don't necessarily bring happiness. There's more to life than … and the rest. But think about it this way.

Life is change so things will never stay exactly the way we would like them to be. Things will always be adapting, growing, improving, ageing and wearing out. Even happiness will change. It will never stick around for ever. It will always be coming and going. And that coming and going may not be an even split. As we all know, bad days are not always followed by good days. Sometimes we experience a string of really crap days that last for weeks, months or even years. There's no pattern, no certainty and no hope of sustainable happiness.

But that's fine. If you let it be. You see, we don't need sustainable happiness, greater happiness or happiness that sticks around a bit longer. That's not what we're really looking for anyway. What we really want is lasting fulfilment, satisfaction and joy. The great news is, that's something we can make happen. It's something we can control. It's something we can all achieve. But to achieve it, first we need to be comfortable with discomfort. That's the how.

You see, happiness occurs when life goes our way. It's accompanied by feelings of pleasure, comfort and pleasantness. In contrast, unhappiness occurs when life refuses to give us what we want. It's accompanied by feelings of discomfort and pain. I'm sure you don't need telling this. But life will not always go your way. So discomfort and pain are inevitable. At bottom, you're left with two options: resist the pain and discomfort, or embrace it. I recommend the latter.

But don't get me wrong. I'm not suggesting you actively seek out pain, or inflict it on yourself. What I am suggesting, though, is a different approach towards pain: acknowledge it, welcome it and let it be. How? Focus on the sensation of pain in the body. Stay with it. Don't try to avoid it. So if you have a knot in your stomach, then focus on that tense, uncomfortable feeling and explore it. That's the way to transform it. And if life is going well, embrace that pleasure too – without clinging to it. Because when we hold on, we become tense. Joy has no tension in it. It's a total acceptance of life as it is in each moment.

> *Joy is love for what is and unhappiness*
> *is love for what is not.*

Be very clear: joy is love for what is and unhappiness is love for what is not. In other words, joy is not about trying to make life perfect. It's seeing that life is perfect as it is. So rejoice in pleasure and pain, sunshine and rain. And allow life to be as it is. That's the way to a joyful life.

CHAPTER 50

Knowledge

We all want knowledge. We want to know tomorrow's weather, what that person is thinking, or how to be a success. Knowledge is a valuable commodity and we're willing to pay good money for it. The right knowledge can quite literally save your life. It can protect you from the wrath of uncertainty. And it can land you a well-paid job.

The trouble with knowledge is, it's not constant. Like everything else in life it's always changing. For example: the round earth superseded the notion of a flat earth. And Einstein's theory of relativity superseded Newton's view of the universe. It seems that whenever we think we've hit the bottom, another level reveals itself. Each level is useful, that's for sure, they act as stepping-stones. But, understand: the bottom line is, there is no bottom line. There's no fixed truth and no end to learning.

We all want to appear knowledgeable. How many times have you been in a class or meeting and been reluctant to admit it when you don't know something? Especially if it's a thing you think you should know.

In karate I see it all the time. Ask students if they know a particular sequence of moves and nobody wants to admit it when they don't have a clue. Heads drop, they look away and carry on as if they didn't hear the question. Sounds obvious, but unless they are willing to admit it when they don't know they'll never be able to learn. The students think they're getting away with it, but they're only fooling themselves, not the teacher.

So why are we so reluctant to admit it when we don't have an answer? Well, from early childhood we get rated for knowing stuff, and berated for not. Self-esteem is built on knowing things. Watch the most confident people in a group discussion and you'll notice they're the people with the most knowledge. No knowledge, no comment. No comment and you fade into the background. Not a big deal, perhaps, if you're enjoying a meal with a group of friends. But career-limiting if you're trying to impress the boss.

> *The aim is to have enough knowledge so you don't have to look up to anyone. And sufficient so you know not to look down on anyone too.*

But let's not get ahead of ourselves. You see, there's more to life than pursuing and parading knowledge. As with all things, we need to strike a balance. The aim is to have enough knowledge so you don't have to look up to anyone. And sufficient so you know not to look down on anyone too. But if you're having trouble looking straight ahead at people, instead of up or down, then the following may help.

Collectively as human beings we know a vast amount of information about the world we live in. But, the more we learn, the more we discover we don't know. Each bit of new information brings up another question. And there are some big unanswered ones. Ask enough questions and you'll soon get to a dead-end. There will always be stuff we don't know.

Understand: knowledge loses its power when you disarm it with questions. So never allow a more knowledgeable person to make you feel inferior. And, conversely, never allow yourself to feel superior towards people with less knowledge than you.

CHAPTER 51

Luck

Flip a coin and what do you get? Probability tells us it's equally likely to fall on heads or tails. Flip a coin a hundred times and what do you expect to see? Most people expect to see an even split of heads and tails. That's approximately what I saw. But what I didn't expect to see was 15 heads in a row. If I were 'willing' heads, I'd be thinking I'm the master of the universe. And if I had put money on heads, during that run, I'd be thinking I had a valuable skill.

But we forget, I know I did, that a 50 per cent chance of getting heads or tails doesn't mean you're going to get an even distribution. Heads will not always follow tails. But when we get a string of repeated outcomes, we find it hard to believe it's random. So we conclude that we made it happen, not that we're lucky. Or more to the point: if things go our way, we're quick to take credit. And if they don't, we're quick to blame others.

Deep down we know we can never be sure about some things. And those things are not limited to the flip of a coin. Life is full of situations that have uncertain outcomes. So we routinely confuse skill with luck.

For example: you read a share-trading newsletter. It makes a string of great predictions. You earn a packet and recommend the newsletter to your friends. They follow the advice and lose a fortune. Was your good fortune due to the skill of the writers or luck? Or take this example. You join an online dating agency. You have a string of bad dates so you conclude the agency is not very good. You warn your single friend to steer clear of the website. She ignores your advice, signs up and meets her future husband. Is the agency bad or was it you?

Succinctly put: when things go our way, we see patterns where there are none. Then we create explanations for these perceived patterns. And make misguided decisions based on our reasoning. And when things don't go our way, we blame other people. So we don't see our mistakes as mistakes, and we don't learn from them.

> *When things go our way, we see*
> *patterns where there are none.*

Our ability to spot patterns and draw conclusions can help or hinder us. Without it we'd see no correlations between our actions and outcomes. There would be no rules for success, and no reason to plan. But, on the other hand, our sensitivity to patterns makes it difficult for us to recognise luck. It's a tricky situation.

But understand this. Life is never certain. So we will never know for sure if our actions will lead to successful outcomes. But, be very clear, we can be sure some things will happen with regularity. For instance: if you step out of a plane, you're going to hit the ground. If you bite your tongue, it's going to hurt. Likewise, when it comes to living a more fulfilling life, if you take wise action it's going to make a difference.

But, most importantly, understand this: if you experience a string of failures in life it might not be your or someone else's fault; it could be the randomness of life at work. So don't take it personally, think life is unfair or that it's punishing you. Don't let bad luck depreciate your self-worth. Remember: the world isn't unfair, it is what it is. The unfair part is your interpretation.

CHAPTER 52

Mastery

To master anything takes time, focus and energy. It's a long and arduous road. In fact, it's a never-ending road. And it's more of an ideal than an actuality. There's always a higher level to which you can aspire. So why bother? For some the motivation comes from the need to be recognised as an expert, be the best, or gain respect from others. But there's more to mastery than a coveted title, and it has rewards far beyond status.

Understand: to master the 'outside' world you need to master your 'inside' world. In other words, you need mental discipline. And that's exactly what the pursuit of mastery develops: a strong will and determination. It's a strength that serves you well in all areas of your life. It has the power to free you from your impulses, bad habits and emotional strife. But be very clear, in the end it isn't a craft or skill you master – it's yourself.

In a sense, every one of us is a master. That's because to learn how to speak, read and write you had to go through the process of mastery. You might not have been aware of this process when you learnt your mother tongue. But you'll know exactly what I mean if you learnt a foreign language as an adult. It's awkward at first. You mix tenses. You struggle to find the right words. But with perseverance and repetition it becomes easier. In time, the words come naturally.

To master any craft, task or skill you have to go through the same process. It takes hours of practice often with slow or little visible progress. But improvement comes with persistence. In a sense, mastery is just another word for persistence. You need to tolerate hours of repetition. You've got to keep going – even during the dull moments. At times you'll feel like giving up, especially when you hit a plateau. But even if there are no visible signs of progress, trust the process – you are improving. So hang in there. More often than not a plateau is followed by a spurt of learning. And as you get better at the task or craft the process becomes more pleasurable.

> **You have to be willing to endure an uncomfortable stage.**

Real satisfaction can be found in the process of mastery. And there's always something you can aim to master in life. But before you begin, be aware: you have to be willing to endure an uncomfortable stage. There's no escaping the boring stretches of time on the path. There are no shortcuts. It's going to take commitment. But remember, the benefits of this process far outweigh the distractions that might tempt you to give up.

CHAPTER 53

Non-attachment

Contrary to popular belief, non-attachment has nothing to do with having stuff and everything to do with your opinions about what you have. For example: if you possess a fair amount of money there's nothing wrong with that, but you'd be attached to it if you couldn't imagine your life without it. The same applies to all of your possessions. If you can't live without them, you're attached to them.

Non-attachment is healthy. The benefits are clear. It gives you freedom. It protects you from manipulative people. It saves you energy and it keeps you sane.

When we take a sober look at the things we become attached to, it's truly bizarre. We become attached to the chair we regularly sit in, the side of the bed we sleep on or even the mug we use. But most people don't believe they're attached to these kinds of things. And I can see why. Let's face it: if you really had to live without sitting on that chair, sleeping on your side of the bed or without your prized possession, you'd soon get over it. But the key question is: 'How soon?'. A good barometer for assessing your level of attachment is seeing how long it takes you to get over something.

But, be very clear, getting over things isn't the same as avoiding them. So if you couldn't sleep on your preferred side of the bed, non-attachment wouldn't mean sleeping on the couch – avoiding the situation. That would be detachment. Non-attachment would be staying in the bed, relinquishing your preference and not complaining about it. You see, non-attachment involves a shift in attitude.

Now that might not be much of a revelation when applied to your preferences. But it is revolutionary when applied to your thoughts.

Let me explain.

The human mind is full of thoughts and they have the power to drive our behaviour. For instance, some people think it's better to give than receive, so they're reluctant to ask for things when they need them most. Some people think there is perfect love, so they feel resentful about one relationship after another. Some people think they shouldn't have to feel pain, so they develop pain-avoidance strategies that prevent them from making healthy decisions.

The trouble is, we don't give our thoughts a second thought. We don't realise we're attached to them. And we don't see how they run our lives. But there is a way out, a path to non-attachment, and it's through awareness and learning to let go. That doesn't mean you should try to stop your thoughts, or crowd out the negative ones with positive thinking. You just need to understand that thoughts are not things. You don't need to hold on to them, and you don't need to let them hold on to you.

> *Thoughts are not things. You don't need to hold on to them, and you don't need to let them hold on to you.*

You'll know when you're making progress along the path of non-attachment because your thoughts and preferences won't have a strong emotional pull on you. But you need to be realistic, because you'll always be attached to some things; for example, your body or life. All you really need to do is keep your attachment to objects, thoughts and preferences to a minimum.

Last word: it's wise not to become attached to people too. Now that might sound cold. But, understand, non-attachment to a relationship doesn't mean creating a distance, being disconnected, or having one foot in and one foot out. That's detachment. It means being fully committed without letting your self-worth or happiness depend on the other person. It gives the relationship room to breathe and a chance to flourish.

CHAPTER 54

Peace

Peace of mind comes not from wanting to change or control things, but from simply accepting them as they are. However, acceptance isn't apathy. It isn't lack of interest, enthusiasm or concern. It means acceptance of the way things are, at this moment, without feeling resentment, frustration or irritation.

Acceptance gives you the experience of true peace. It frees you from worry. You see, when you get worked up you make problems bigger than they really are. So instead of worrying, control what you can control then sit back and let life unfold. There really isn't much more you can do to help some situations. But you can make matters worse if you spend your time complaining about what's not right. Understand: peace of mind comes from knowing that life will not always be totally in your control. Sometimes you have to let go of the reins and let life take over. There is tranquillity to be found in that attitude.

Peace ends when you become overly emotional. Make no mistake. There's nothing wrong with having strong emotions *per se*. But if you want a healthier and more fulfilling existence on this planet it helps to learn how to stop yourself from being swept away by them. Awareness can help. With awareness you can observe your emotions. You can become a detached observer, free from their strong pull. To develop this ability notice what is happening in the moment. Label or report your behaviour, thoughts and feelings as they happen. Say to yourself: 'I am feeling angry/irritated/upset/like a mug'. Then notice the body sensations that are accompanied by these thoughts. This approach to emotional events leads to better decisions and more constructive behaviour. But it takes practise. So don't be hard on yourself if you understand the reasoning but can't put it immediately into action. Take it step by step, little by little, and improvement will come with perseverance.

When we pay attention to the present moment we find peace. We free ourselves from worry, judgement and the striving to arrive. In a sense, the things that we don't pay attention to don't exist for us. Out of sight, out of mind. And out of our world. Perhaps that's why people bury their heads in the sand when they want to escape unpleasant experiences. But this isn't about avoiding life's difficulties. It's about looking them squarely in the eye and saying: 'I see you', then responding appropriately. Be very clear: reacting in an unbalanced way is the fastest route to losing your state of tranquillity.

> *When we pay attention to the present moment we find peace.*

Remember: there is a part of you that is perfect, tranquil and calm. It's untouched by the storms and strong winds that sweep over you in life. So when things become too much to manage, take refuge deep inside. Connect with your pure awareness. It's at the core of your being that you will find the clarity of mind you'll need to improve your situation. Peel off the layers of your habitual thoughts and attitudes. Take a fresh perspective. Reframe. That's the way to a more peaceful existence.

CHAPTER 55

Power

P ower is often misunderstood. Mainly because the people we notice with power are the ones who abuse it. But power can be a force for good. Put power into the right hands and it can lead to positive change. For example, parents use their power to influence their children's characters and development. Leaders use power skilfully to advance the interests of their organisation. Sales people influence their customers' buying decisions. When we see power as the ability to influence we see it in a more positive light.

> *Power is good for your health. You need it to make positive changes in your life.*

But power isn't just about other people, it's also important for your own sense of well-being. You see, power gives us a sense of control over our environment. And as many psychological studies have shown, people with a sense of control are healthier and live more satisfying lives. Conversely, when people are put in a position of little control they become stressed and less confident. Put simply: power is good for your health. You need it to make positive changes in your life. So don't give yours away easily.

For some people the thought of standing their ground and fighting for power is enough to make them cringe. The pursuit of power isn't for everyone. We all have a different level of need for it. Some people enjoy influencing others to get things done. Others just want a quiet life and are happy to do what they are told. Most people hate to fight. They shy away from conflict situations. So if you can handle conflict, you're at an advantage over your peers if you aspire to be a leader.

But even if you don't aim to be a leader or great influencer it's wise to protect yourself from those who might try to abuse their power over you. For example, in personal relationships we sometimes have to deal with people who try to manipulate and exploit us. And at work we often have to face bosses and co-workers who try to use us like pawns. So be prepared. Here's how.

In general, you give your power away when you become too concerned with other people's opinions. Sure it's important to build a good reputation and manage other people's perceptions. But when we try too hard to please others, or look good, we leave ourselves open to abuse. To protect yourself: form your own opinion of yourself. Don't let others determine your self-worth. Remember, genuine confidence comes from within, and so does genuine power.

> ### *Don't let others determine your self-worth.*

And if you do aspire to be a leader or influencer, understand: a person with compassion wields more power than a person with muscle. In karate you learn power is not in being strong, but in the right use of strength. And there's more power in an open hand than in a clenched fist. And I'm not talking about a chop over a punch. When used compassionately power is a formidable force. It has the potential to make life better for many people.

CHAPTER 56

Purpose

What's the point? Is there a point? Few people live without having some thoughts about why they exist. Perhaps we won't ever get a definitive answer to those questions. But in the meantime we can use what we know to get the most out of life.

Research suggests becoming who we can be and giving something back are the top ways to feel most fulfilled in life. The trouble is, few people know who they are let alone what they can become. Most people are so influenced by other people's opinions that they lose sight of who they are as a person. Then, on top of that, they become influenced by social norms or accepted ways to live and work. You know: the steady job, steady income, steady relationship and so on. Soon our life becomes so steady it doesn't move. It becomes stagnant. It lacks purpose and passion.

Everybody has something to offer the world; however, you're the only one to decide what that is – not your teacher, parent or spouse. Perhaps you already know what your purpose is, but through lack of support or encouragement you've given up on living it. Nevertheless, just as you shouldn't be expected to live your life pleasing other people, don't expect others to do as you please. When you commit yourself to a path, if it's right, life will provide you with the support you need. So don't hold back. Remember: we can all make a difference.

> *When you commit yourself to a path, if it's right, life will provide you with the support you need.*

So, if you lack purpose beyond paying the bills, now is your time to find it. You see, your purpose may be hidden but that doesn't mean it can't be found. You just need to know where to look for it. And the best place to start is in the past. Look back to times when you've felt deeply satisfied and fulfilled. What were you *doing*? What were you *being*? Come up with enough examples and soon you'll see a pattern. You'll notice there are a handful of activities that allow you to be a certain type of person, and feel great about it. That's the clue to discovering your talents.

Now, once you know your talents your task is to develop the best of them. So if you can write well, work on writing. If you can teach well, work on teaching. If you can entertain well, work on entertaining. Then find a way to deploy your talents in the world for the good of others. You see, purpose is about giving and getting. And, as I'm sure you know, there's more satisfaction to be gained from giving to other people than only getting for yourself.

That's purpose in a nutshell. Discover. Develop. Deploy. I'm talking about your positive and most beneficial talents, of course.

CHAPTER 57

Success

Do you remember what you wanted to be when you were a child? I do. Back then, to me, anything seemed possible. I wanted to be a musician, actor, performer, doctor, but least of all a writer. But age gradually narrowed those options as I realised potential and passion were more important than possibility.

Then, out of the blue, age struck again. Possibility transformed into an ugly beast – impossibility. And this time, as with my age, potential and passion weren't on my side. I was 30 with a career-limiting injury and never going to be a world karate champion. That was it. Full stop. But how could that be? I had the talent, desire and drive. I had trained with the best, fought the best, but I was never going to be number one in the world. I'd missed the boat. Put simply: I would never fulfil my potential.

In vain, I tried to appease myself with the reasons why it never happened. But it still hurt. In my eyes, I had failed. And no learning from my mistakes was going to help. When you've missed the boat, you've missed the boat. It's not that I thought I was a total loser. I could've listed a string of achievements that would make any mother proud. But at that stage in my life, I didn't fully appreciate this.

Success isn't about getting something – a title, fame or financial security. It's about going after your dream with all your heart (and your head) with the reassurance that if you don't achieve it, you'll always have something to offer. With this mindset there's little room for disappointment. You see, whether you hit the target or not, you'll always have something to give. Sure, in my case it was too late to learn from mistakes and try again. But it wasn't too late to show others how to avoid them.

Look at it this way. Genuine success isn't about the prize; it's about who you become as a player. That's the crux: you don't take part to prove anything – being the best, world champion or whatever. You take part so that one day you can demonstrate what you've become. And your demonstration will be your instruction. Remember: behaviour is contagious. The excellence in you will nurture the excellence in others. Whether you're the world number one or not, you'll be the boost of confidence others need. You'll stimulate the if-he-can-do-it-so-can-I mentality.

> *Genuine success isn't about the prize;*
> *it's about who you become as a player.*

Understand, if there's a sure route to success then it's this: find your talent, develop it, and offer what you've become in the process to the world, for the good of others and yourself.

CHAPTER 58

Time

Time is a mystery. You can't see it, touch it, hear it or smell it. But most people believe in it. They think there's a grand clock 'out there' that keeps the correct time. When, in reality, there is no such thing. In fact, time is no-thing. But in our world, it's everything. Our entire existence is organised around time.

When we take a close look at time we see that it's a construct of the human mind. It's nothing more than a concept, an idea, to describe the process of change. Think about it. How do we count time? We count it by observing the changing sun, moon or solstice. But these 'comings' and 'goings' don't fit into equally spaced units, so we fudge the figures to impose an order on a world that's not as ordered as we'd like it to be.

For instance, each lunar month lasts about 29.5 solar days but we tinker with the days in a month so we have 12 months in a year. We say there are 365 days in the year and by this we mean that it takes the earth 365 days to circle the sun. When, in fact, it takes 365¼ days. This means every year we gain a quarter of a day. So, again, we tinker with the figures and every four years we put the extra day into our smallest month, February. Literally: we make time up.

Time might not be real, but it really does matter. In fact, most of us wouldn't get much done without time. In all senses of the word we need a deadline. We need the fear of not making it, the fear of running out of time before we can make the best use of it. But time has other benefits. It makes it easier for us to communicate, coordinate and come together. It's a measure of progress. And it's a great healer too.

Time certainly has its uses. But if you're not careful, it can start to use you. You see, for most people there's too much to do and not enough time. So instead of feeling motivated by time, they feel the pressure of it. For others, there's not enough to do and too much time. So instead of feeling they have free time, they get bored and suffer from having too much of it. We think that's just the way it is but time doesn't have to be experienced that way. You don't have to be used by the hours, minutes and seconds.

You see, time is a product of the mind. Change your mind and you change your perception of time. So drop time urgency thoughts: 'Time is running out', 'There's not enough time' and so on. And stay in the present: if you're eating then just eat. If you're thinking then just think. That's the way to escape the chains of time.

> *Time is a product of the mind. Change your mind and you change your perception of time.*

And if you think you've got too much time on your hands, stop fighting against it. Pause. Let go of striving. Move out of the flow of time. Remember: you might have less to *do* but there's always more you can *be*.

Understand: what we crave is not to have more time or less of it. What we want is to be free of it. So step outside the illusion of time but continue to live with it, free of its ability to control you.

CHAPTER 59

Values

What do you value in life? For some, it's family and friends. For others, it's the freedom to choose and independence. We all value something. And often we find that our life naturally gravitates towards what's most important to us. But sometimes we let other people's opinions and expectations pull us away from what we care about most. We're strange creatures. We'll even go into debt to get the things to impress the people we don't like. But if we're not true to our values, we'll never feel fulfilled.

What's more, often we find ourselves doings things because it's what other people want for us. For example, you may have had parents who thought it was important to pursue a particular career. So they encouraged you to follow a certain path. Perhaps you didn't want to disappoint your parents so you did what they said. And now you find yourself hating your job or profession. Far too frequently we try to please others and lose sight of what we want to do. Then we end up feeling miserable and unfulfilled.

Understand: no matter what you do or where you go, any action you take is to fulfil a need. If the action you take is successful and your need is met, you feel pleasure. If you're unsuccessful, you feel pain.

Take food, for example. It's a basic need. We all have a need for survival and eating helps. To fulfil that need you may decide to work. And, if you do, the work you choose will be to fulfil a higher need. You might have a need for recognition, say. Not a pat on the back from the boss, but a need to see your face on a screen, in papers and so on. And if you had an interest in music, and a good voice, you may consider a career as a singer because that would increase your chances of being in the public eye.

But if your need for recognition was not being fulfilled in any other areas of your life, and it was a very strong need, you may be tempted to pursue a quick fix. You might do something that goes against your values but fulfils your need. The point: sometimes your desire to fulfil a need can pull you away from your values. A need will always have a stronger pull than a value. But they must both be aligned for optimum fulfilment in life.

> ### Sometimes your desire to fulfil a need can pull you away from your values.

Are your needs aligned with your values? If not, what factors are contributing to the misalignment? Consider the severity of any mismatch and what steps you can take to address it. Identify your pivotal needs and align them with what you think is most important to you in life. Then use that information to guide your decisions and actions. Remember: life will always be more satisfying when your needs and values are aligned.

CHAPTER 60

Wisdom

Wisdom is the pinnacle of human development and, unwittingly, it's the last chapter in this book. But what exactly is wisdom? It isn't easy to define. In fact, there isn't a consensus of opinion on what constitutes wisdom, but most people agree that it's important. Perhaps we'll never be able to define wisdom in a concise way. But that doesn't mean it's fluffy or idealistic. As I hope this book has demonstrated, wisdom is down to earth and has practical implications for everyday life.

Each one of us has an intuitive understanding of what wisdom means and what it looks like. The challenge, however, is to turn wisdom-related knowledge into action. This isn't an easy task. None of us was born wise. Wisdom is developed from experience and practice. So the older a person is, the more likely they are to be wise. But at the same time, wisdom isn't measured by the number of grey hairs on our head. It isn't bestowed upon us in old age. Like most other human qualities it has to be acquired through application and a willingness to change.

As we get older wisdom helps us to prepare for physical decline and ultimately death. But why wait until you're on the home straight until you acquire wisdom? Most people spend

their youth trying to obtain knowledge. And I can see why –
we all want to live the best lives possible. And knowledge can
help in that pursuit. But we fail to understand: knowledge is
necessary to master the outside world, but wisdom is what we
need to master our inner world. Simply put: if our insides are
in turmoil, intellectual knowledge is of little help.

> **Wisdom has to be acquired through
> application and a willingness to change.**

Sure, knowledge can help you to make informed decisions
about how to improve your inner life. But it's the ability to
take that knowledge, put the parts together, and see the bigger
picture that counts. You see, wise people have perspective.
They gather information so they can see from more than
one point of view. They know what counts and what to
ignore. And they get to the core. And they understand acquiring
knowledge is an important aspect of wisdom. But, crucially,
they also understand intelligent people are not always wise.

Something else about 'knowledge'. The wise understand all
knowledge is open to question. So they give up the belief in
absolute knowledge. Skilfully, they balance the notion that
there's no bottom line without falling into a bottomless pit.
In other words, they know there are more ways to look at
things than they can possibly imagine. So they're reluctant to
jump to conclusions or preach their knowledge as the truth.
They recognise there are many things they don't know. But
they're able to use their current understanding to lead the best
possible life. At the conclusion of this book, I hope that's the
case for you too.

About the author

Dean Cunningham is a personal development coach, a former British karate champion and international athlete. He graduated from the University of London with a Bachelors and Masters degree in Economics and studied Japanese at Keio University in Tokyo. His career as a consultant in the field of people performance began with Arthur Andersen (acquired in the UK by Deloitte in 2002) and led to him establishing his own business as a professional coach. He can be reached at: **www.deancunningham.co.uk**.